Famous Biographies for Young People

FAMOUS
AMERICAN SPIES

by Rae Foley

Dodd, Mead & Company · New York

5/51

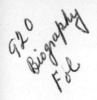

Eighth Printing

Printed in the United States of America
by Vail-Ballou Press, Inc., Binghamton, N.Y.

FOR LILLIAN BRAGDON
who shares my love for Connecticut's
hills and valleys, for its changing
skies and seasons

CONTENTS

WHAT IS A SPY?

𝒯HE ACTIVITIES of spies are a part of the secret history of nations. It is upon intelligence* supplied by spies that battles have been won and, in more than one case, the whole course of a war has been changed.

How essential the work of a spy becomes is indicated by Napoleon's comment: "One spy in the right place is worth 20,000 men in the field."

There have been spies as long as there have been wars. Colonel McDougall, superintendent of Britain's Royal Military College, Sandhurst, said: "Without accurate intelligence of an enemy's movements, the greatest military talent is useless."

Before a general can send his men into the field he must know what the enemy's forces are, how they are armed, what supplies they may have, where they come from. To acquire this information he needs someone within the enemy lines who can learn the facts and then—more difficult—get them into the general's hands.

Of all occupations known to man that of the spy in wartime is probably the most dangerous. The soldier in the field has the support of his army. The spy is on his own. The es-

---

* Intelligence, as used in this book, means any information about troop movements, armaments, supplies, battle plans, or morale of the enemy.

9

sence of his hazardous job is that his identity is concealed, the true nature of his work unguessed. Often he lives in disguise. "By the law of war," said Sir Thomas Barclay, "a spy is liable, if caught, to the penalty of death."

That is why the spy has turned to the use of codes, ciphers and secret inks. That is why he has learned to transmit his messages in the handles of knives and in hollow eggshells; why he hides them in the notes of a musical score or even in the embroidered pattern of a dress.

Why do people become spies? What kind of people are they? The people whose adventures are told in this book volunteered—for no one can be ordered or forced to become a spy—because of a great love for their country, a love that was stronger than their feeling of self-preservation. Few of them received much financial reward. Fewer still received public recognition of their risk and sacrifice. Some of them not only paid their own expenses but gave everything they had: fortune, friends, life itself. These men and women believed that a way of life was worth risking all that they had in order to maintain it.

Some of them, of course, had a strong love of adventure and excitement. The thrill of outwitting the enemy made them look without fear at "the bright face of danger."

What kind of people were they? All kinds, from silversmiths to professional detectives, from society women to shoemakers, from lawyers to young boys and even a seventeen-year-old girl.

There are people whose activities were suspected from the beginning. There are people whose identity was not discovered for a hundred and fifty years, so well was their secret kept.

For if the spy is to survive, his secret must be kept. From the time when he embarks on his mission he is alone, dependent on his wits and his courage. There is not one minute in which he dares to forget that discovery means death.

It was a long, long time before we had any organized spy service. In fact, many people still believe that the United States has never used spies. The Military Intelligence Bureau known as G-2 did not come into existence until the First World War. The Secret Service did not function until 1865. Its chief purpose was to aid in uncovering counterfeiters and smugglers. Before that time, the gathering of intelligence was done, for the most part, on an amateur level, both in the Revolution and the Civil War. In the Civil War, the government departments and the generals had their own personal secret agents. In the Revolution, George Washington, in desperation, begged for men to bring him the information he needed. In fact, the Father of his Country helped to devise many of the methods they used. And before the Revolution, in the years when the Colonies were stirring into revolt, the people themselves created their own Underground, as people were to do 150 years later in invaded countries in Europe.

It is with that Underground movement that the story of America's famous spies opens, to the sound of galloping hoofs.

THE REVOLUTION

PAUL REVERE, WARNING BELL
OF THE REVOLUTION

*T*HEY CALLED him "Bold Revere." Almost any day he might
have been seen hurrying along the streets of Boston, a rather
short, stocky fellow with dark hair and ruddy cheeks. He had
discarded the leather apron and trousers of his apprentice days
but his nails were broken and his hands scarred from his
work as a silversmith.

He was the oldest son of Apollos Rivoire, a French Hugue-
not who had come to the Colonies to escape religious perse-
cution and here had changed his name. Paul was probably
born during the last days of December, 1734. According to
present-day standards, he had a difficult childhood. Beyond
a few years at a "writing school" he had no education. At a
time when today's boys are barely getting into their stride in
school, he was apprenticed to a silversmith. He worked long
hours that would horrify us, but he took them for granted. In
time, he was to make himself the finest silversmith in America,
producing works of great beauty.

To a young man like Paul, energetic, ambitious, self-con-
fident, the days did not seem long enough. Life was a great
adventure and he wanted to experience all he could of it. Un-

like the men who headed the Revolution, he was not primarily a thinker. He was a man of action. He wanted, first of all, to master his craft. He wanted, next, to become a wealthy and prominent citizen. He wanted, finally, to play an active part in his world. All these things were possible in the Colonies. All of them he achieved.

Men lived fast in those days, shouldering heavy responsibilities at an early age. When Revere was nineteen, his father died, leaving him the chief support of his mother and six younger brothers and sisters. At twenty-one, he had already served as a second lieutenant in the French and Indian Wars.

In his spare time, he learned to make artificial teeth, for which there was a great demand in the Colonies. Of course, he did not claim that people could actually eat with them, but at least they would fill up the ugly gaps in their mouths. Some years later, during the Revolution, he was to identify the dead body of his great friend, Dr. Joseph Warren, by the teeth he had made for him. This was the first time on record of such an identification being made, though it is common now in criminal investigation.

Paul Revere married twice and had sixteen children. In true American fashion, he managed so well that in time he was able to send several of them abroad to complete their education and to have advantages which he had never known.

While he was working as a silversmith and building a reputation as a fine craftsman, he found time to take an interest in what was going on around him. The Colonies were in a ferment. There was growing discontent over British rule. The Tories preferred things as they were. The Whigs wanted change. Revere became a Whig and in time met and knew well many of the men who were to head the revolutionary movement in Massachusetts: Sam Adams and his cousin John, James Otis and John Hancock, Dr. Joseph Warren and Dr. Benjamin Church.

For a while he listened to their talk. But Revere was not a man to be satisfied with talk. He wanted action. So he joined the Sons of Liberty, which, in a way, was to become the first espionage network in America.

Today, a secret agent would be horrified by the amateur methods of the Sons of Liberty. To begin with, they held all their meetings quite openly at the Green Dragon Tavern. In the second place, they knew one another. In the modern world, every effort is made to prevent a spy from knowing the identity of any other, for his own protection. But the worst feature of all was that one of the leading Sons of Liberty, who attended the meetings and knew their plans and secrets, was actually a traitor, slipping away after each meeting to make his report to the British Governor Gage. But it was a long time before they knew that.

When, in 1768, the British brought troops down from Halifax, not to protect Massachusetts but to act as a police force, the Sons of Liberty became an Underground movement. They kept a cautious eye on the Redcoats, checking their actions, watching where they stored their supplies. But they bided their time.

It was not until 1773 that they really went into action. That was when the British government passed the Tea Act. This gave the East India Company, which was on the verge of bankruptcy, a monopoly of the American market. It also gave the Whigs a rallying cry. People who had been divided now found a common cause.

At the Green Dragon Tavern, Paul Revere and the Sons

17

of Liberty made secret plans. The tea was not to be unloaded in Boston harbor. They would see to it.

The first tea ship arrived. There was a bustle at the Green Dragon, whispers, smothered laughter, grunts. Anyone looking in would have seen a group of men, young and middle-aged, putting on Indian disguises and daubing their faces. Like boys playing a game they grunted, "Me know you," as they identified themselves to one another.

Then a war whoop rang out, the first warning bell of the Revolution, and Revere and his friends raced down to the wharf. They were a gang, perhaps, but an organized gang. While some of them stood on guard, with musket and bayonet, the others boarded the tea ship, hoisted out the chests of tea and dumped their contents into the water. It was back-breaking work and the men struggled all night long. Dawn broke before they had finished.

> Our Warren's there and bold Revere
> With hands to do and words to cheer

wrote an admirer next day.

Most of the "Indians" straggled home to bed, weary but triumphant. There was to be no sleep for Paul Revere, however. That very morning he was chosen to be the man who carried an account of the Boston Tea Party to New York and Philadelphia. This is the first record we have of Paul Revere "riding express" for the Committee of Correspondence. But this was the role that was eventually to make him famous.

At that time, the only safe and quick method the Colonists had of keeping a link with each other and exchanging news was by sending mounted men to ride express. As the British began to maintain a closer check, it became more difficult to get a permit to leave Boston. Nevertheless, Revere made the ten-day ride between Philadelphia and Boston many times. He was keeping the links between the Colonies strong and firm.

Along with his taxing job as silversmith and his frequent absences on his rides for the Committee of Correspondence, Revere took on a volunteer job. "I was one of upwards of thirty," he wrote later, "chiefly mechanics [artisans], who formed ourselves into a committee for the purpose of watching the movements of the British soldiers, and gaining every intelligence of the movements of the Tories. We held our meetings at the Green Dragon . . . In the winter, towards spring, we frequently took turns, two by two, to watch the soldiers, by patrolling the streets all night."

They strolled casually around Boston. Because they were in their own city, there was no reason to question their movements. Everyone knew them. If they did arouse suspicion among the Redcoats, they knew every nook and corner. There were alleys in which they could conceal themselves. Best of all, there were houses of their friends in which they could take refuge in case of need, secure in the fact they would not be betrayed.

As a result of this constant espionage, they kept informed of troop movements and the plans of the British. So when, in 1774, they learned that Gage was going to send two regiments to Fort William and Mary at Portsmouth, New Hampshire, Revere mounted a fast horse and started on a sixty-mile ride. It was bitter winter weather. His horse slipped and slid over snow and ice. When he reached his destination, half frozen, hungry and exhausted, his horse was "nearly done," as a friend later described the arrival.

Because of Revere's warning, men in "gundalows" rowed down the river to the fort and took it by surprise. The fort surrendered. The men, wading in icy water up to their waists, removed the arms and powder kegs from the fort, leaving it helpless. Much later, the gunpowder was said to have been used at Bunker Hill.

Back from his wintry ride, Revere set to work with the Sons of Liberty to make the life of the British in Boston as miserable as possible. Watch as carefully as they could, the Redcoats found their stores were constantly being damaged or disappearing altogether. If they loaded a boat with bricks, it sank. If they piled a cart with straw for the cavalry, it turned over. Guns vanished from a battery at Charlestown. Artillery in Boston was damaged or it disappeared completely.

There was a certain gun shed over which a British sentry stood guard. One night, the sabotage crew stole up to the rear of the shed and pried off planks, careful not to make the slightest sound, and crept inside. They took the barrels off the guns and shoved them outside, carrying them off to a schoolhouse, whose teacher was a Son of Liberty. Later, they made wooden mounts for the guns for their own use.

All this was a maddening business for the British who were helpless at coping with the Revere spy ring. They strolled around Boston as easily as in their own back yards. However carefully the British laid their plans, there were eyes to watch them, ears to overhear them.

By day, Paul Revere and the other Sons of Liberty were respectable merchants and craftsmen, teachers and lawyers and doctors, going openly about their business. But by night, they became illusive gadflies, making life as unpleasant as they could for the British, destroying their supplies, undermining their morale, yet apparently invisible.

But while the Sons of Liberty seemed to be immune, uneasy rumors reached them. One day, Revere met a friend on the street. The latter startled him by repeating, word for word, remarks that had been made the night before at a secret meeting at the Green Dragon Tavern. Revere discovered that Governor Gage was being informed of all the plans of the Sons of Liberty. That could mean only one thing. One of them was a traitor. While they were spying on the British, the British had a spy among them.

Revere could not understand it. The Sons of Liberty took a solemn oath at each meeting to reveal nothing, except to their leaders: Dr. Joseph Warren, John Hancock or Dr. Benjamin Church.

Naturally, one of the first of the Sons of Liberty to attract the British suspicions and attentions was the man who carried messages from Boston to New York and Philadelphia and other trouble spots. Paul Revere himself. "The noted Paul Revere," one Tory called him. And when he went to New Hampshire for a meeting of the Provincial Congress, a British leader reported glumly: "Paul Revere went express thither. It portends a storm rather than peace."

It was getting harder and harder to leave Boston, now that the British—thanks to the traitor—knew Revere's identity. But, with ingenuity and probably some amusement, he continued to outwit the enemy, though the latter were now quartered all over Boston. Some of the officers were even billeted in the houses of active members of the Sons of Liberty. In one way, this created a problem, because they had to be even more cautious than before; in another, it proved to be an advantage, as it helped them to watch the movements of the enemy. Also, by keeping their ears open, the Sons of Liberty learned a lot from careless comments dropped by the officers from time to time.

The watchful eyes of the Underground never slept. So on April 14, the patriots observed signs of activity. Gage seemed to be preparing for troop movements. Boats were being lowered from the man-of-war *Somerset* into the Charles River. That meant the troops were going to cross the river. They would do that only if they were expected to march to Concord where the patriots had stored artillery, ammunition and supplies of food. And in Lexington, between Boston and Concord, were Samuel Adams and John Hancock, men with a price on their heads. They must be warned of their danger.

Dr. Joseph Warren, physician, patriot and President of the Committee of Safety in Boston, sent for his reliable express rider. On Sunday, the sixteenth, Paul Revere set off to carry the warning. We know little of that ride, except for its results, but, in importance, it was as valuable as the "midnight ride" that made him famous.

All we can guess is that there was no sound of galloping hoofs this time. Revere would have ridden slowly, so as not to attract attention, careful to avoid the Redcoats, appearing to have no particular errand. In any case, he served as a warning bell. Immediately, the people of Concord set to work moving off the cannon to new places, putting bullets in sacks to sink them in the swamps, burying musket balls. Provisions of flour and beef, of rum and molasses, of rice and candles, were carefully hidden.

Because of Paul Revere's warning, Gage's purpose in marching on Concord was defeated before the troops ever moved from Boston.

While he was in Lexington, warning Hancock and Adams of the likelihood that the British were going to advance, Revere also saw Colonel Conant, who was in command of the Minute Men.

"I agreed," he said later, "that if the British went out by water we would show two lanterns in the North Church steeple, and if by land one as a signal."

On Tuesday evening, the eighteenth of April, the watchers observed that soldiers were beginning to gather at the bottom of the Common. The British troops were preparing to move. So alert was the spy network that three different people came to Revere's house to bring him the news.

About ten o'clock, Dr. Warren sent for Paul Revere and begged him to set off for Lexington at once to carry the alarm. He had already dispatched another messenger, William Dawes, down Boston Neck on horseback. Revere was to cross the Charles River.

As the *Somerset* had been moved into the very mouth of the river to guard it and to prevent anyone crossing, this was no easy job. On top of that, thanks to the traitor in their ranks, the British were prepared to stop Revere if he did manage to get across the river. They had Redcoats on horseback waiting in ambush on the other side and all along the road to Concord.

Revere made his way cautiously along the dark streets to the house of Robert Newman, the young sexton of the church. There were British officers quartered in Newman's house, so the young man had yawned and climbed the stairs to his room, pretending that he was going to bed. Then he climbed out of the window onto the roof and got down to the ground as quietly as he could.

Paul Revere met him. The British, he whispered, were going by water. Newman nodded. He crept into the church and got two lanterns. Up he climbed to the top of the belfry, which was visible from across the river. He lighted the lanterns and hung them out.

The signal given, Newman hurried home and scrambled up on the roof again and in his bedroom window. There the angry British arrested him. He was the sexton, he had keys to the church. He had signaled to the enemy.

Newman was all indignation. He had gone early to bed. If they wanted proof, let them ask their own officers who had been playing cards downstairs at the time. The British officers who were billeted in the house backed up his story. Newman, they agreed, had not left the house that night.

Meanwhile, Revere had to get out of Boston to carry the alarm to Lexington. By now the troops were falling in rapidly. No one was to be allowed to leave the city. Here his familiarity with the byways of Boston helped him out. In the darkness he slipped away to the river bank where, some time before, he had hidden a boat. Two friends were waiting to row him across.

As boats from the *Somerset* were being loaded with troops, it was dangerous enough to cross the Charles River that night. Sounds carry over water. There must be no conversation, no splash as the oars entered the water. No sounds at all. But— they had nothing to muffle the oars.

A moment's consternation. Then, as Revere's children told the story in later years, one of the men slipped out of the boat. In the dark he ran to the house where his girl lived. He whistled softly. An upstairs window opened. A head was thrust out. A few whispered words. Then something dropped from the window, the young man seized it and ran for the boat to muffle the oars. It was a flannel petticoat. "Still warm," Paul Revere said.

Past the sixty-four guns of the *Somerset* the boat crept. "It was then young flood, the ship was winding, and the moon was rising," as Revere described the scene. A quiet landing on the Charlestown side. Revere hastened to the home of Colonel Conant. Yes, they had seen the lanterns. Revere told them "what was acting and went to get me a horse."

He swung into the saddle and started for Cambridge, the quickest route to Lexington. The moon shone bright. It lighted the road. It also lighted the cockades and holsters of lurking British officers, waiting in ambush for him.

A tug on the reins. Revere turned his horse and galloped back, turned onto the Medford road, and soon outdistanced his pursuers, riding headlong straight into history.

> A hurry of hoofs in a village street,
> A shape in the moonlight, a bulk in the dark,
> And beneath, from the pebbles, in passing, a spark
> Struck out by a steed flying fearless and fleet;
> That was all! And yet, through the glow and the light,
> The fate of a nation was riding that night.

In Medford, he awakened the captain of the Minute Men and after that "alarmed almost every house till I got to Lexington."

As though they had been waiting for that warning bell, the farmers for miles around roused to action. The Minute Men, who had kept their guns within reach of their hands since his first ride, set off to spread the alarm. Farmers abandoned their plows and reached for their muskets. Teachers set aside their schoolbooks, took up their powder horns, and began to walk, heading for their first encounter with the British Regulars. Through the night men marched, quickly and firmly, ready to take their fate into their own hands.

By midnight, Revere reached Lexington and rode to the parsonage of the Reverend Jonas Clark, where Hancock and Adams were staying. One of the watchful Minute Men had noticed British officers loitering on the road and had called eight volunteers to guard the parsonage. The family had gone to bed when Revere rode up and demanded admittance.

He was refused. The family must not be disturbed by any noise.

"Noise!" Revere exclaimed. "You'll have noise enough before long. The Regulars are coming out."

After that, he had no difficulty in rousing Hancock and Adams. He told them "what was acting" in Boston. By the time he had finished his story, William Dawes, who had come by way of Boston Neck, arrived.

Together, the two messengers started for Concord. Dawes and a young man whom they met on the road stopped to arouse a household and Revere rode on alone.

He was stopped by four Redcoats who aimed their pistols at his breast.

"If you go an inch farther you are a dead man."

They forced him into a pasture or "his brains would be blown out."

Revere was not unduly alarmed. Then there was the sound of a distant shot.

"What was that?" his captors demanded.

That, Revere explained boldly, was a warning signal. The whole countryside was aroused. The British plans were known.

They released him but they took away his horse and Revere

returned to Lexington on foot. He never got to Concord that night. Neither did Dawes, who was in such a hurry and so excited that he fell off his horse. But Revere's earlier warning had sufficed.

"The bells rang," a British officer reported, "and drums beat to arms in Concord and were answered by all the villages round."

The Battle of Lexington, that moved from Lexington to Concord and back that night, was only a minor skirmish of the Revolution, but it was prophetic of the end. The first shot "heard round the world" heralded the beginning of the American fight for independence. A handful of farmers and mechanics that night opposed a large force of trained soldiers and drove them off in defeat. One out of nine men sent out by Gage failed to return. More ominous, one out of two officers had been picked off by men who were undisciplined soldiers but dead shots. And, most infuriating, there was no trace of the arsenal or the provisions which the troops had come to seize. Paul Revere and the Underground had done their work well.

Revere, now on foot, returned to the parsonage and accompanied Hancock and Adams to a place of safety, though Hancock wanted to stay and fight. Then Revere went to the tavern where Hancock had left a trunk filled with papers that would have cost his head if found by the enemy. With a friend's help he managed to get out the trunk and conceal it.

Next day, Dr. Benjamin Church, that ardent Son of Liberty, who was a fiery Whig, showed Revere his stockings splashed with blood. He had been in the thick of the fighting, he said. Now he had to get back to Boston at once. And to Boston he went.

By chance, one of the Sons of Liberty saw him leaving Gage's headquarters. After that he observed that the doctor, who had always complained of being short of money, had a pocketful of British guineas. The doctor, high in the councils of the Sons of Liberty, had from the beginning been the traitor in their midst. He was the man who had reported the activities at the Green Dragon Tavern to the British.

With the opening shot of the Revolution, Paul Revere found himself with other jobs besides that of riding express. He seems to have had a quality of Yankee ingenuity that enabled him to turn his hand to many things. For instance, he was asked to cast copper plates and make money for the colony. So, for six months, he did this.

Then George Washington discovered with dismay that there was practically no gunpowder available. At once, Revere was sent to Philadelphia to learn, from the best mill, how to make it. The mill owner didn't want competition. All he would consent to do was to walk Revere through the place as fast as possible, not letting him question the men or examine the machinery. But Revere used his eyes and his wits to good advantage. Later, a man was able to get into the factory and secure the necessary information, and for months Revere manufactured gunpowder.

In 1777, Revere was sent to Worcester to bring back the British prisoners taken by General Stark at Bennington. For the next few years of the war, after the British withdrew from Boston, he must have found the time rather dull. As a lieutenant-colonel in command of Castle Island he had little to do.

It was in 1779 that he became involved in the Penobscot affair, the one dark spot on his record. There was a small garrison at Penobscot, which the Americans were ordered to seize. The British had few men, the Americans a large force. An odd little fleet, made up mostly of Yankee privateersmen, and commanded by Dudley Saltanstall, was to attack. On board the vessels were 1,200 militiamen commanded by General Lowell.

The privateersmen were independent and had already caused Washington a great deal of annoyance and trouble. They disliked orders. They obeyed only when they wanted to. This time, they did not want to. There was a clash between the land and naval forces. The land troops wanted to attack. The privateersmen said no. Men were landed and then—the ships sailed away and left them to take to the bushes.

It was an unnecessary and shameful defeat. Saltanstall was court-martialed and cashiered. Paul Revere's reputation suffered, as he seems to have agreed with Saltanstall's action. What really was his part in this affair? Was he still Bold Revere?

Revere himself fought doggedly for a court-martial that would examine his case and clear his name. It took years, but at length he succeeded.

". . . the whole army was in great confusion," read the conclusions of the hearing, "and so scattered and dispersed that no regular orders were or could be given."

With the end of the war, Revere returned to the making of his silver and, as our Navy grew in importance, he built a mill to roll copper for ships and public buildings. He became a prominent citizen and a wealthy manufacturer, who could educate some of his children abroad. He could pay his workmen more than the standard rate, because he knew the importance of having satisfied workers.

We hear of him twice more in relation to his country. When the Federal Constitution was up for ratification by the Massachusetts Convention in 1788, Samuel Adams was dissatisfied. It did not, he declared, completely meet his wishes. A meeting of mechanics was called at the Green Dragon Tavern and afterwards they marched to Sam Adams's house to demand ratification. At their head marched Paul Revere. Adams listened to them and cast his vote for ratification of the Constitution of the United States.

In 1812, war again broke out between the United States and Great Britain. A group of 150 North End mechanics volunteered to build fortifications for the defense of Boston. The name that headed all the rest was that of Paul Revere. He was then eighty years old, hardly able to perform heavy labor. But still, to the very end, he remained Bold Revere.

ENOCH CROSBY,
KNOWN AS "THE SPY"

*T*HE OPENING shot of the Revolution at Lexington may not have been, as the poet claimed, "heard round the world." But it was certainly heard in Danbury, Connecticut.

The first person in Danbury to enlist after the Battle of Lexington was Enoch Crosby. He had been born in Harwich, Massachusetts, in 1750. Because his father was too poor to provide food for all his children, Enoch left home at sixteen and set out on his own. Almost the only way to obtain training and employment was to be apprenticed in some trade. Enoch was apprenticed to a cordwainer [shoemaker] in Phillipstown, now Kent, Connecticut, and remained there until he was twenty-one.

At that time, he was nearly six feet tall, broad-shouldered, powerful and athletic. He had also, as was to appear later, a quick mind, great courage and an ability to make vital decisions at a moment's notice.

Enoch was twenty-five when he heard of the embattled farmers at Lexington. For some time he had been carrying on his trade of cordwainer in Danbury. Now he was the first to join Captain Benedict's regiment, which was ordered to St.

31

John, a British post in Canada.

"We were now," Crosby recorded later, "in full view of the enemy, who kept up a constant cannonading, which only caused us to dodge now and then, merely seeming to get us in a fighting mood. We were soon ordered to advance; but had only proceeded a few rods, when we were attacked by a body of Indians in ambush; who, after a short contest, were glad to show us a specimen of their speed in running."

Some time during his enlistment Enoch fell ill and was taken to a hospital. The doctor assured him that he was not well enough to return to action. Crosby assured the doctor that he was. He insisted on returning to duty.

"To my great satisfaction," he wrote, "I was one of the number that marched into the fort to the tune of Yankee Doodle, and took charge of the prisoners."

Periods of enlistment were brief in those days and, when his had expired, Enoch went back to shoemaking and slowly recovered his health.

All through the Revolution, but particularly in the early days, the Colonies were bitterly divided among themselves. There were, perhaps, an almost equal number of Loyalists who still remained steadfast to the King, and those who sought complete independence. But, worst of all, there was no sure way of telling where any man stood. A man who had been a neighbor for years was now under suspicion. Was he friend or foe?

When his health was restored, Crosby decided to enlist again at Carmel, New York, and he set out to report to the American camp at Kingsbridge. In Westchester County he encountered a stranger who, it turned out later, was an ardent Tory. They settled down to talk. Walking alone was a solitary business.

"Are you going 'down below'?" the stranger asked.

Now at that time the phrase "down below" referred to the British army, while the Colonials were known as "the upper party."

Crosby answered that he was.

The other man brightened. Crosby, he explained, need go no farther. A group of Loyalists in the vicinity were forming a company to join the British army. He could go with them.

If young Crosby was startled by the mistake, he gave no sign of it. At once he realized that he could get information of great value to his side. To discover the identity of the secret Loyalists was of vital importance to the safety of the country.

So he turned back with his new friend. He questioned him closely about this company: its personnel, its plans, its meeting place. The Loyalist readily answered all his questions. Within a short time, Crosby knew the names of the Loyalists who planned to enlist. He also knew the names of many others in the community.

This information was needed by the Committee of Safety and it was Crosby's job to get it to them. Not far from White Plains there lived a Mr. Young who had some association with the Committee of Safety. Crosby made his way there and poured out his story. Mr. Young promptly took him to the Committee of Safety. The man in charge was John Jay, who, at that time, was beginning to build a spy ring of his own. Many years later, he was to tell James Fenimore Cooper the story of that spy ring. Out of it Cooper drew material for America's first great novel, *The Spy*, of which Enoch Crosby was to be the hero, under the name of Harvey Birch.

John Jay listened to Crosby's account, meanwhile summing

up his intelligence, character, physical strength. He asked Crosby if he would lead a company of Rangers * to the place where the Loyalists held their meetings.

Crosby hesitated. He was willing to do as he was asked, he explained, but he had enlisted and he was expected to join his company at a certain time. That was all right, Jay assured him; he would explain to Crosby's captain why he was late in reporting.

In fact, John Jay did not want Crosby to report to the army at all. The young man had performed a valuable service in running down the Loyalist company and discovering the identity of other foes to the country. Would he devote himself to uncovering other Loyalists?

Crosby had a hard decision to make. This was the service his country required of him and he knew how useful, indeed how necessary, it was. On the other hand, he could succeed only if he passed openly as a Loyalist, as a traitor to the cause in which he believed with all his heart. It meant that his friends would scorn him, that his own family would be deeply grieved and shamed.

If he hesitated, it was only for a minute.

"We will furnish you with a pass for your protection," John Jay told him, "but it must never be exhibited save in the last extremity. Should you be arrested as the emissary of the enemy, you shall be secretly furnished with the means of escape."

So Crosby chose with open eyes the lonely path of the spy. From this time on, there was nothing to help him but his own quick wits. His greatest danger was capture, by his own side.

* In the Revolution, Rangers were mounted men who were always on call to go anywhere.

He was now Crosby the Loyalist.

He informed the Rangers about the secret meeting place of the Loyalists and then returned, alone, to join the latter. The Rangers closed in and arrested them all, including Crosby, and marched them off to jail in White Plains.

That night, he "escaped" from the jail. There was much banging of muskets, much running about, as the soldiers tried to "capture" the prisoner. There must be no doubt in the Loyalists' minds that Crosby had really escaped.

Creeping through the shelter of a patch of corn, Crosby made his way back to Mr. Young's house to plan his next move.

He was provided with a peddler's pack containing a set of shoemaker's tools and he set off, pretending to be looking for work. What he was really looking for, of course, was Loyalists.

He wandered around, using his trade as his excuse to knock at the doors of farmhouses. Even when people were not in want of shoes they were usually eager to talk to a stranger and hear news of what was going on. It was often weeks before word of a battle could reach them.

At one farmhouse, where he asked for a bed for the night, the farmer's wife said that he could stay if he would be willing to make a pair of stout shoes for "our John." The shoes had to be able to stand a lot of wear. Crosby pricked up his ears. "Our John," he learned, was going into the British army.

Crosby, busy working on the shoes, was much interested and surprised. Going into the British army, was he? But where could he join?

Oh, that was easy. A Loyalist company was being formed not three miles east of there. The obliging farmer offered to introduce Crosby to the Tory captain.

The captain was eager for recruits and urged Crosby to enlist. Crosby hesitated. He wanted to enlist, he said; nothing he would like better. But he wanted to fight side by side with his friends, not get in among a lot of strangers. Were any of his friends in this company?

The captain opened the muster roll and let Crosby read all the names on the list. He studied it carefully, getting it by heart. Then he returned it regretfully. Sorry, there was no one he knew in this company. He'd try to find one in which his friends had enlisted.

The captain hesitated and then said that there were a few names he hadn't shown him. Some Loyalists were afraid to have their names on record. He kept a special list of these people, which, for their safety, was concealed under a large stone in the meadow. The captain took Crosby to the big stone and showed him these secret names. He also indicated that the Loyalist committee was to meet in his parlor at nine the next evening.

Late that night, when the family was asleep, Crosby slipped out of the farmhouse and hastened as fast as he could to White Plains to make his report. Hours later, he crept back into the house and was sound asleep in bed when he was called the next morning.

That evening at nine the Committee gathered to discuss their plans. At ten o'clock, the house was surrounded by the American Rangers. The Committee scattered in a panic, some hiding in the attic, some in the cellar. Crosby got into the spirit of the thing and hid in a closet from which the Rangers dragged him forth.

The Loyalists were manacled in pairs and marched off to White Plains. From there they were sent on to Fishkill to be examined. A whispered word told Crosby that he must go along as a prisoner but that some way would be found for him to escape.

Next day, the prisoners marched twenty-five miles to Peekskill. And here Crosby had one of his most painful experiences, though it was one he had known he could not avoid for long.

As he was marching, handcuffed to a Loyalist, he passed an elderly man who had formerly been his teacher and was a close friend of his father's.

The teacher was thunderstruck. Enoch Crosby, his former pupil, his friend's son, a traitor!

What, he asked, was the meaning of this?

Crosby looked him in the eyes. "I have no explanation to offer."

He walked on with the Loyalist prisoners, head high, but sick at heart. Within a few days, he knew, his father and mother would know that he had been arrested as a traitor to his country.

An old church in Fishkill was used as a prison. Here the Committee of Safety came to examine the prisoners. They looked at the evidence, the muster roll and other papers that Crosby had managed to procure. There were some signs of amusement as the Committee members watched Crosby standing before them, apparently in the throes of fear. They looked at him suspiciously and held him for further questioning after the other Loyalists were marched back to their prison.

When he was alone with them, the Committee broke down and laughed. They discussed the best method for him to "escape" this time. There was a window in the extreme northwest corner that was partly hidden from the outside by a willow tree. That would be his best chance to get away. There was a possibility, of course, that something might go wrong. For his own safety, they could not let the soldiers who guarded the prison know who he really was. If there was a little loose talk, the Loyalists would soon know the truth about him.

However, he was to do his best, and when he was out of prison he was to report to a certain man at Wappinger's Creek. From now on he was to be John Smith. Actually, before he had finished his career as a secret agent, Enoch Crosby had a number of aliases: John Smith, Levi Foster, John Brown, Jacob Brown.

When the other prisoners were asleep, Crosby prowled cautiously around the dark interior of the ancient building, with its low ceiling, its thick walls, its small arched windows. There was a soldier stationed at each of the four corners of the church.

Cautiously he raised the window they had mentioned. He pulled himself up and through the window. For a moment he listened to the tramp of the guards' feet as they patrolled. Then he let himself fall, in the soft darkness, into loose mould. He realized what it was—a newly made grave. Through the graveyard he hastened, half running, half crouching. A sentry heard him and challenged him sharply. Crosby leaped for the swamp which would conceal him, while shots flew around him.

Once he had shaken off his pursuers he set off for Wappinger's Creek. An informant there told "John Smith" that an English officer was enrolling men for a Loyalist company, but it had been impossible for him to learn any more. Crosby wandered on, stopping at farmhouses, asking idle questions, learning nothing about the company.

At last, he reached the house of a farmer who was so cautious about what he said that Crosby's hopes rose. This man must know something.

The suspicious farmer finally agreed to let Crosby stay and work on the farm. He didn't need any one to repair shoes but he did need a man to kill hogs. A spy usually learns that he has to be prepared to do all sorts of unexpected things, so Crosby agreed to kill hogs.

He had worked for several days, not daring to rush his questions until he had won the farmer's confidence. Then he said that, while he didn't mind killing hogs, what he really wanted was to join an English company and fight the rebels. The trouble was that he did not know of any safe way of doing it.

Oh, if that was all! The farmer knew just the thing. Not far away, in a curious little cave on the west side of a mountain, an English captain had been hiding while he recruited a company of Highlanders. The farmer knew all about it. In fact, he had been supplying him with food.

Crosby immediately asked to enlist. He told the sympathetic farmer about being captured with an English company and how he had managed to escape.

That night the two men set off in the dark for "the cave in the mountain." At the base of the mountain the farmer stopped near a clump of dwarf cedars. Behind it was a huge rock, with a deep cleft in the middle. The farmer struck the rock with a heavy stick. After a moment a ray of light showed through the cleft in the rock.

A man's voice spoke and the farmer answered. Then he introduced the new recruit as "John Smith, a faithful friend of his Majesty."

The two men doubled up and crawled through a tunnel

39

behind the rock into an open space, which had been fixed up like a room with a table, seats, food. Here the farmer left Crosby, who remained behind with the English captain.

For several days Crosby stayed in the cave while the captain waited for the rest of his men. They were to leave in three days' time, he said, and to meet at the home of a Loyalist whom Crosby referred to only as Mr. S.

He had all the information he needed now but he did not know how to get it into the hands of the Committee of Safety in time to prevent the new company from marching off.

The captain unintentionally gave him a clue. He suggested that the Loyalists all meet at a certain place. Crosby objected that this would be dangerous. If they were all together they could easily be captured. Suppose they separated for the night and met the next day.

There was no way for him to get to the Committee, but there was a friend not far away who could make the trip for him. Crosby hastened to the friend's house where he wrote this letter:

"I hasten this express to request you to order Captain Townsend's Company of Rangers to repair immediately to the barn, situated on the west side of Butter Hill, and there to secrete themselves until we arrive, which will be tomorrow evening, probably about 11 o'clock, where, with about 30 Tories, they may find, John Smith."

The friend took the letter, saddled a horse, and set off at a gallop to reach the Committee.

Next night, the Loyalist company gathered at the barn at which they had agreed to meet. They had been riding far and they were tired. They settled down to rest and to sleep. All but Crosby.

He waited, his ears straining, listening to all the noises of the night. At length, he heard someone cough outside the barn. He coughed in answer.

The barn doors were flung open and the Rangers came swarming in. "John Smith" pretended to hide in a haymow, but the Rangers did not know who he was, and when half a dozen bayonets were jabbed into the haymow he came out in a hurry.

Captain Townsend remembered his face. This was the man who had escaped from the church-prison in Fishkill. He wasn't going to escape again. While the other Loyalists were marched back to the church, which was beginning to seem familiar to Crosby, he was to be placed where he would have no chance of escape.

Of all places in the world the one in which Townsend decided to imprison his captive was the home of John Jay, the Chairman of the Committee of Safety, for which Crosby was working!

As it happened, Jay was not at home. No one was there but a pretty maid who recognized Crosby at once but gave no sign. Townsend placed his most reliable sentinel at Crosby's door, after locking him in. This time the traitor was to be kept safe.

A few hours later, the pretty maid brought out a bottle of Jay's brandy and offered Townsend a drink. He was delighted. So was the sentinel when the maid went to see him. Before long, both men were in a drugged stupor. The maid took their keys and released Crosby. In a hurried whisper, she told him which way to go.

He shook his head. "You'll be in danger for this."

She smiled. "I'll put the keys back," she assured him.

She couldn't, however, unfasten the heavy shackles he wore

41

and he had to move slowly and awkwardly until at last in a thicket he managed to get rid of them. This, by the way, is not the only case of people escaping from handcuffs in Revolutionary times. Apparently, they were extremely heavy but they must have been fairly simple to remove.

When Townsend awoke from his drugged sleep the next morning he was wild with anger. For the second time this Loyalist had escaped from him. There would be no third time, he vowed. Next time, he would kill the man.

It was late in the year now and the pack on Crosby's back must have seemed heavy as he trudged down the snow-covered roads, a man who had everyone's hand against him. He drifted from farm to farm, sometimes stopping to make shoes and ask questions, sometimes driven off by suspicious people who were afraid and distrustful of strangers.

In November, the daylight fades early, and it was after dusk when he saw a light flickering in a window, one evening. The Tory owner admitted him and agreed to let him sleep there. He had hardly settled down before there was a bang at the door. Two men came in, muskets in their hands, hunting for Loyalists. They searched the house. Then they saw Crosby.

"I saw that man taken prisoner at Fishkill prison," one of them said. "You're a traitor. Jay is determined to make an example of you."

Crosby must have wished that Jay had been less thorough in his desire to protect his spy's real identity.

Prodding him with their muskets, the Americans drove him out before them. Crosby had seen their expression and he knew that they were not going to wait to turn him in. They intended to see that he never escaped again. Once out of sight of the house, he opened the lining of his vest, tore out his secret pass from the Committee of Safety and identified himself. There must have been considerable surprise on their part, but they let him go.

On Crosby went in the dark until he reached another Tory house. His own people were against him; here, at least, he was welcomed. Or so he thought.

The Tory opened the door and stared at him. "I know you. You betrayed us to the Rebels. My company was seized. Leave this house!"

Crosby went out into the dark and the cold again. Both sides were hunting him now. It was late when he reached a farm where he was allowed to be sheltered for the night.

In the morning, he got in touch with a member of the Committee who ordered him to return to Wappinger's Creek. At the house of a kindly Dutchman there he could work quietly at his trade. He was to remain until he received further orders. He was to take the alias of Jacob Brown.

On the third day he received a letter. He was to report to the Committee at Fishkill. There was a long consultation. Crosby was becoming too well known in the vicinity. He escaped from prison too easily and too often. He had better work somewhere else for a time. So he was ordered to meet John Jay at the home of a Dr. Miller in the village of Hopewell.

The doctor kept a drug shop in his house. When Crosby got there a number of people were waiting for Dr. Miller, who was away.

A pretty, smiling girl came up to Crosby. "Dr. Miller's opiates, you recollect," she told him in a low voice, "are wonderfully powerful when mixed with brandy."

He recognized her then as the maid who had helped him

escape from John Jay's house and who had drugged Captain Townsend.

While Crosby waited for the doctor he listened to the talk of the people around him. He realized that they were discussing him and his exploits, that he was regarded as a contemptible traitor who had gone over to the Loyalist cause.

"Have you ever seen him?" Crosby asked, breaking in on the conversation. He stood looking down at the other man from his full six feet.

"A little slender artful-looking fellow, about five foot three," the other answered promptly.

There was a stir at the doorway and John Jay himself came walking in. His eyes fell on Crosby, but he passed on without recognition. Crosby drifted out of the shop and stood patting Jay's horse until Jay himself came out.

"Too many people," Jay muttered. "Go back to the Dutchman's. We'll have to plan another meeting."

At a later meeting Jay told Crosby that he was to be sent north to Bennington, Vermont, where, according to rumor, people were enlisting in a Tory regiment.

It was 125 miles to Bennington, through cold and severe storms. Crosby made the trip, chilled to the bone. Little is known of his exploits there except that he detected a number of enemies and had them arrested. But, considerably to his surprise, it was while he was in Vermont that he heard rumors of enemy activities at Pawling, New York, not far from his old home in Danbury.

Back rode Crosby and prowled around Pawling until he discovered some members of the Loyalist company. He followed his usual plan, and offered to enlist with them. He discovered, too, that the Tories were holding secret meetings near a Quaker meeting house on Quaker Hill, on the east side of Pawling.

Crosby was in real trouble. If he sent for the Rangers and the rest of the Loyalists were arrested while he escaped, the Tories would be suspicious of him. If he were to be arrested by Captain Townsend of the Rangers he was as good as a dead man. He sent word of his predicament to the Colonel of the Rangers who knew him in his real role.

The meeting of the Loyalists was held, as scheduled, behind the Quaker meeting house and the Rangers surrounded and arrested them. Before Townsend could put outraged hands on Crosby the Colonel rode up.

"I can't walk," Crosby declared, staggering. "I am much too lame."

"You shall be carried, tied on my horse," the Colonel answered roughly.

As they came closer to the jail, the Colonel dropped behind and told Crosby in a low tone how to escape. Just as the prisoners began to be marched into the building, and the guards were busy watching them, Crosby slid off the Colonel's horse and got away unseen.

Over and over, the same thing happened. Crosby enlisted, had the company captured, and then escaped. At length, he had been seen too often. The game was up. The Tories knew him at last for what he was—an American spy.

For many, many months he had worked tirelessly, always in danger, always alone. The service he had performed was of inestimable value to his country but now he could no longer perform it. He was allowed to retire and he returned to his brother-in-law's house. Now the truth could be told and he was cleared with his family and friends and neighbors. Instead of being ashamed, they were proud of him. He was safe and he could rest. Or so he thought.

But if the Colonial troops now regarded him highly, the Loyalists hated him. He had done them incalculable harm. Company after company of their soldiers had been arrested before they could fire a single shot at the Rebels. Many Loyalists had been unmasked and the Colonial government knew who they were. Crosby might be done with them, but the Loyalists were not done with Crosby.

One evening, he was sitting in his brother-in-law's house when a shot was fired through the window, grazing his neck. After that, he knew that the war was not over for him. He slept with a loaded musket at his side.

A few nights later, the door was broken open. Armed men rushed into the room. They beat his brother-in-law almost to death for harboring him. Then they came into the room where Crosby had been sleeping. He reached for his musket and exchanged shots with the man in front. They grappled with each other and Crosby, who had immense strength, got his enemy on the floor. He had him at his mercy.

Then two men seized his arms and a third aimed a pistol at his breast.

"No," one of them cried, "let us pound him to death."

When they had finished with that terrible beating, Crosby lay unconscious on the floor and they left him for dead. They went through the house, plundering it, opening every drawer and closet, breaking or stealing everything they could get their hands on.

It was months before Crosby recovered from that brutal beating and was strong enough to get around again. Then, as

46

soon as he could walk, he went out to enlist. He took a subordinate command in the Marquis de Lafayette's corps.

Apparently, even the gruelling months of danger and the beating that had so nearly killed him failed to destroy Crosby's zest for living or his sense of fun.

Once while he was on duty he decided to "afford a little sport for his soldiers." There was a British sloop-of-war coming up the river. Crosby sent one of his men, noticeable in Lafayette's uniform, to parade the beach, while he concealed himself back of the beach in the woods with five men.

The enemy saw that lonely soldier. The bait was attractive. They swallowed it. A boat with eleven men and a lieutenant put off to capture him.

The soldier paced along the beach and then, imperceptibly, moved closer and closer to the woods. Once out of sight, he took to his heels.

"Come on, my boys, we have them!" Crosby shouted, laughing.

His five men rounded up the twelve prisoners and marched them to Fishkill and the old Dutch church-prison, which had a familiar look to Crosby, who had spent a lot of time escaping from it.

When the war was over, Enoch Crosby returned to civilian life. He served as a justice of the peace and as a deputy sheriff. In time, the government gave him the sum of $250 in payment of his wartime services as a secret agent.

Many years later, when Crosby was an old man, James Fenimore Cooper's novel, *The Spy*, was made into a play and produced in New York. Curiously enough, Cooper himself never knew the name of the spy whom he called Harvey

47

Birch, but by this time all America knew it. On the opening night, Enoch Crosby sat in a box to watch the performance and before the curtain went up on the play, the audience wildly applauded the man who was the true hero of the story.

NATHAN HALE,
MARTYRED HERO

$\mathcal{G}$ENERAL GEORGE WASHINGTON sat in his temporary headquarters, writing a letter. The quill pen scratched across the
paper.

"As everything, in a manner, depends on obtaining intelligence of the enemy's motions," he wrote, "I do most ear-
nestly entreat you and General Clinton to exert yourselves
to accomplish this most desirable end. Leave no stone un-
turned, nor do not stick at expense, to bring this to pass, as
I was never more uneasy than on account of my want of
knowledge on this score."

Do not stick at expense. That showed how important the
matter was, because there was little money to spare and every
penny had to be stretched as far as possible. But, some way or
other, he must know what the enemy was planning. Otherwise, he could not decide how to move or what to do.

Washington's appeal brought no answer. In desperation,
the general called a council of war. Some trustworthy and intelligent person must be sent, in disguise, into the British camp
on Long Island. What Washington needed was a man who
had military training and knew how to use his eyes, a man

49

whose judgment he could trust, whose report would be accurate. Above all, he needed a man brave enough to be willing to enter the British lines.

The council agreed that a spy must be sent to Long Island. But where was such a man to be found? Washington sent for Lieutenant-Colonel Knowlton. Could Knowlton find the right man for him?

Knowlton called in a number of his officers and explained what was needed. There was a pause. He asked for volunteers. Another pause. A longer one. He turned to one of the silent officers.

"Will you volunteer?"

"I am willing to go to fight them," the man replied, "but as for going among them and being taken up and hung like a dog, I will not do it."

A voice said, "I will undertake it!"

It was the voice of Captain Nathan Hale, who was haggard and weak from a recent illness, but standing firmly enough.

There was consternation among the officers, for everyone knew and liked Nathan Hale. He must have been a young man of exceptional charm, for he was immensely popular; people who once knew him never forgot him, and he had a long-reaching influence over his friends.

Both Nathan Hale and his brother Enoch had been in the class of 1773 at Yale College. Among the members of that class was Benjamin Tallmadge who, like Nathan Hale, and perhaps because of him, was to become a key part in Washington's spy service.

At Yale, Nathan had been interested in sports, running, and wrestling, and particularly jumping. There was a tradition that he could stand in an empty hogshead and jump from it into the next one and the next, right down the line. He was also prominent in the literary society and took part in the school plays.

After his graduation from Yale he began to teach school in a poor little building equipped only with a few primers and spellers, and without so much as a blackboard.

From there he went to the Union School. He must have had boundless energy, because school hours were long and yet he was able to carry on an extra class for young ladies on summer mornings, from five to seven.

When the war came, he enlisted for a year, but at the time for re-enlistment, many of the men decided to go home. The war seemed to drag on and on. Their farms and families needed them. There was almost no money.

Nathan wrote in his diary: "Promised the men if they would tarry for another month they should have my wages for that time."

It is no wonder that a woman, recalling him many years after his death, said: "Everybody loved him. He was so sprightly, intelligent and kind—and *so* handsome."

By this time, however, it is unlikely that he was quite so handsome. During that year of service with the third company of the Seventh Connecticut Regiment, he had not only been under fire, as captain of his company on Long Island, but his face had been scarred by exploding powder.

After the meeting in which he had volunteered to go into the enemy lines as a spy, his friends gathered around young Nathan, urging him to change his mind. It was one thing to fight the enemy face to face. But to risk being "hung like a dog" was another.

"I think," Hale said, "I owe to my country the accomplish-

51

ment of an object so important and so much desired by the Commander of her armies, and I know of no mode of obtaining the information but by assuming a disguise and passing into the enemy's camp. I am fully sensible of the consequences of discovery and capture in such a situation."

The consequences! The consequences of being caught were death. His friends grew more emphatic.

"Who," one of them demanded, "respects the character of a spy?"

Nathan took his time in replying. Then he said: "For a year I have been attached to the army, and not rendered any material service, while receiving a compensation for which I made no return."

Then this very young man summed up better than anyone else the answer to those who are contemptuous of spies:

"I wish to be useful, and every kind of service necessary for the public good becomes honorable by being necessary."

His friends were silenced. Nathan Hale had made up his mind. They could do nothing more.

Today, of course, we see how mistaken this whole situation was. Colonel Knowlton had openly asked a whole group of officers to serve as secret agents. Nathan Hale's offer to perform the job had been openly made. So a number of people were aware in advance of what he was going to attempt and how he was going to do it. But that was one of the first uses of spies by General Washington and it was necessarily an amateur attempt.

Nor did the mistakes end there. When Hale set off on his journey he was provided with no possible means of getting his information back to his commanding officer. He was given no assistant with whom he could get in touch, to whom he could turn for help. The only aid he was given was "a general order to all armed vessels to take him to any place he should designate."

Colonel Knowlton—some historians say George Washington himself—explained to young Nathan what was required. The American Army had managed a successful retreat from Long Island, which was now controlled by the British. It was essential for the Commander-in-Chief to know what the British intended to do.

On a Saturday evening, Hale set off with Stephen Hempstead. The armed sloop *Schuyler* was to take him across to Huntington, Long Island. It was Hempstead, fifty years later, who gave an account of his last glimpse of Nathan Hale.

Hale, he said, removed his uniform and put on a plain suit of citizens' brown clothes, with a round broad-brimmed hat. Apparently he intended to pose as a Dutch schoolmaster in search of work. He gave Hempstead his army uniform, his commission, his papers, and also his silver shoebuckles to keep for him.

It was almost dawn when he landed at Huntington and vanished into the morning mists. Beyond that point we can only guess what happened.

Did he acquire the information Washington so badly wanted? The American Army retreated to Harlem Plains and the British seized Manhattan. By this time, Washington knew what the enemy was up to. There was no further occasion for Hale to expose himself to danger within the enemy lines.

But, whatever the reason, he went on to New York, seeking more information. How he got there remains a mystery. The most likely solution is that he found work on one of the market boats that were ferrying back and forth with fresh vegetables for the army. The British were finding it hard enough to get—and keep—men to load and unload the cargo. This would have been a good cover for the American spy.

Once off the boat, Hale was on his own, inside enemy lines. What information did he collect? We will never know. What we do know is that he carried in his clothes evidence of his activities.

And then he was captured! It seems probable that, in an attempt to leave the city with the information he had acquired, he mistakenly hailed a British boat instead of an American one. It is also possible that a Loyalist saw him and recognized him as an American officer. Another persistent rumor, but one which seems to be without foundation, is that his cousin, Samuel Hale, who was the British army's deputy commissary of prisoners, recognized him and betrayed him.

Meanwhile, there was silence. Not a word had reached Washington's headquarters since Nathan Hale vanished into the mists, a week before.

Then, on September 22, Captain John Montressor of the British Engineers, who was aide-de-camp to General Howe, arrived at the American outpost on Harlem Plains with a letter about an exchange of prisoners. While he was there he told the Americans that one of their officers, a Captain Hale, had been executed that morning as a spy.

There was consternation in the American camp and grief. Lieutenant-Colonel Webb was sent with a flag of truce to the British headquarters to find out what had happened. Later, Nathan's brother Enoch recorded the information that was obtained: "Nathan, being suspected by his movements that he wanted to get out of New York, was taken up and examined by the general, and some minutes being found with him, orders were immediately given that he should be hanged. When at the gallows he spoke and told them that he was a captain in the Continental army, by name Nathan Hale."

Only later did the truth about Nathan's death come out, and then there was raging anger and indignation as well as grief in the American camp. Nathan Hale had been hauled before Sir William Howe who had ordered that he be taken to the execution post and hung up without trial.

Calm, gentle, serene, young Nathan waited in a tent while the gallows were being prepared. He asked for a clergyman but was refused. The provost-marshal who hanged him was a surly brute who, years later, was himself hanged in London for forgery.

"Hale's manly bearing and the evident disinterested patriotism of the handsome young prisoner," wrote a British officer who witnessed the execution, "sensibly touched a chord of sympathy in Howe's nature."

The hanging took place at what is now Third Avenue, between 66th and 68th Streets in New York City. There was a ladder that Hale had to mount to reach the platform from which, with a noose around his neck, he was to jump or be pushed off.

He stood at the foot of the ladder, great dignity in his bearing, his voice gentle and steady.

"I only regret," he said, "that I have but one life to lose for my country."

His body was left hanging and his tongue was stilled forever. But his words have rung down the years. He had nothing to say about his personal bravery. He gave all he had to his country and he gave it gladly and with dignity, without boasting or fanfare.

The martyrdom of Nathan Hale was a needless blunder, but it achieved two purposes: it made other Americans proud of him and eager to avenge his death; it taught the secret agents who were to follow him the importance of having safeguards. And the man who profited most by this was his Yale classmate and close friend, Benjamin Tallmadge, who was to become the key figure in establishing George Washington's spy ring in New York City.

ALIAS CULPER

After the tragic death of Nathan Hale, General Washington decided that a spy ring must be set up that would give him reliable information about the activities of the British in New York City. There were to be no more of the mistakes that had proved fatal. This time, every precaution would be taken.

That spy ring was to prove so successful that the links in the chain that ran from New York City, within the enemy lines, to General Washington's headquarters were hidden for 150 years and only discovered when a tireless research worker named Morton Pennybacker identified the handwriting of the two men who used the alias of Culper, and so uncovered the whole amazing story.

It was Nathan Hale's old Yale classmate and friend, Major Benjamin Tallmadge, of the Second Regiment, Light Dragoons, who established a spy ring in New York City.

Young Tallmadge—he was in his early twenties—was a native of Long Island and he knew New York City well. At Washington's request he set to work to build his chain of secret agents, using the alias of Mr. John Bolton. Later, when a "dictionary," or code book, was established, he became Number 721.

The chief of this spy ring, and the man who had much the most dangerous job, was young Robert Townsend, who stayed in New York City, in the heart of the British camp, all during the war. It was said of Robert that "in his veins flowed the blood of Norman conquerors." He was a descendant of John Townsend, one of the original patentees, who settled in Flushing, Long Island, in 1645.

His father, Samuel, was a Friend, and strict in his religious observances. He was strict with his son, too. Robert, born in 1753, was sent to school when he was only three years old. But his teacher, feeling that he was much too young for books, let him play with the ducks on the pond instead of studying, until he was a little older.

Samuel was a sturdy patriot. For thirty years he was a magistrate, then a member of the Colonial Assembly, the Provincial Congress, the Committee of Safety and the Convention that was considering the first Constitution of the State. All this public service would indicate where his sympathies lay, particularly his association with the Committee of Safety. His Tory neighbors resented his stand and had him arrested as a rebel. He was forced to take an oath of allegiance to King George.

Perhaps because the Tories suspected that the taking of an enforced oath was no guarantee of loyalty, or because his house was a stately and comfortable one, British officers were quartered in his home at Oyster Bay for all the four years of the war. Young Robert managed his father's store in New York City, importing flax and sugar and molasses, tea and coffee and iron. When the war began, he was made a commissary, but after the brigade to which he was attached was defeated, he returned to his former job.

His family, like so many others, was divided in its sympathies. His cousin Hannah married Major Green of the British army. But his pretty sister Sarah, later the heroine of Cooper's novel, remained a fiery rebel. She was to play a small but vitally important part in uncovering the greatest traitor of the Revolution. However, to the British officers billeted in her home, she appeared to be only a charming and mildly flirtatious girl. More than one of them, particularly Colonel Simcoe, the great friend of young Major John André, fell in love with her.

Robert Townsend and his friend, Abraham Woodhull, were the two men who gathered most of the information for General Washington in New York during the Revolution. Townsend remained in the city. Woodhull lived at Setauket, Long Island. Together, they used the alias of Culper in signing their letters. Later on, Woodhull was known as Culper Sr. and Townsend as Culper Jr.

Culper Sr. wrote to "Mr. John Bolton" of his "hope it may be of some service toward alleviating the misery of our distressed country, nothing but that could have induced me to undertake it, for you must readily think that it is a life of anxiety, to be within (on such business) the lines of a cruel and mistrustful Enemy."

All during the war Woodhull paid his expenses for his secret service activities out of his own pocket. More than seven years later, the government reimbursed him for what he had spent.

It was Townsend, Culper Jr., however, who took the greatest risks. He lived in the heart of the enemy camp. There was not a day in which he did not risk discovery; not an hour when he could afford to relax for fear a careless word would betray him.

But the lesson of Nathan Hale's death had been learned.

59

Culper, both senior and junior, declared that if anyone were ever told of their identity they would stop work from that hour. Later, they even refused to meet Washington, who wanted to thank them personally for their great assistance to him. They were going to take no unnecessary risks.

How careful they were is indicated by the fact that, all during the war, Townsend's partner in the store never suspected his activities.

It was Washington himself who wanted Culper to remain in New York because "all great movements and the formation of all intelligence must originate at, and proceed from the Headquarters of the enemy's camp." Townsend, at Washington's suggestion, "put on the airs of a Tory."

About this time Townsend began to collect news for a man named Rivington, the King's Printer, who was publishing a Tory newspaper, the *Royal Gazette*. Now and then, Townsend also wrote editorials for this newspaper, in which he upheld the King's cause and violently attacked the rebels. Not until long after the war was it learned that Rivington had also been playing a dangerous double game, and that he, too, was actually loyal to the Continental government. The strangest part of all, and the clearest indication that this spy ring took no chances, is that Rivington and Townsend seem never to have known that they were on the same side and working for the same cause.

Together the two men financed a coffee house near Wall Street, which became a favorite gathering place for British officers. Townsend found it a useful way in which to meet the officers casually and pick up information. The officers sought out Townsend because they discovered that when one of them got favorable mention in the *Royal Gazette*, he was apt to find himself shortly getting a promotion.

As time went on, Washington discovered that Townsend's information was not only accurate but that it often enabled him to forestall British action. Young Townsend widened his circle of acquaintances among the British officers. He picked up news about supplies and where they came from, about troop movements, about the British defense system.

How useful Townsend's activities were is indicated by a report from Mr. John Bolton: "Some pieces of useful intelligence respecting the movements of the enemy in this late intended expedition to New London, and which I have reason to believe in a great measure defeated their intentions, have been communicated by Culper."

Any day, a fashionably dressed young man might have been seen wandering around the fortifications, looking at carts loaded with supplies, chatting with British officers at that friendly coffee house near Wall Street. All sorts of strange facts came to light in this idle conversation to which the polite young Townsend listened alertly. He was shrewd enough not to ask obvious questions or to betray how deep his interest was.

Here he learned that the British were turning out counterfeit confederate currency and distributing it to the Tories in Connecticut, so they could pay their taxes in worthless money.

The hardest problem that Woodhull and Townsend, Culper Sr. and Jr., had to solve was how to communicate with each other. Townsend was in New York City, Woodhull in Setauket, Long Island, over fifty miles away. Townsend had to get his information to Woodhull, who had to pass it on to Major Tallmadge, who, in turn, relayed it to General Washington's headquarters, where it was seen either by Washington

61

himself or by Alexander Hamilton. And only by them.

At first, they attempted to communicate directly with each other. Townsend went to Long Island or Woodhull came to New York. But this proved to be too risky. On one occasion, Woodhull had come to New York and was carrying a letter back with him for General Washington.

"Soon after I left Hempstead Plains," he wrote, "and got into the woods, I was attacked by four armed men, one of them I had frequently seen in N. York. They searched every pocket and lining of my clothes, and also my saddle, which the enclosed was in, but thank kind Providence they did not find it."

"Not long since," he declared, "there was not the breadth of your finger betwixt me and death."

A better and safer means of communication had to be found. So the other links in George Washington's spy ring were formed. What was needed most was a messenger who could carry intelligence from Townsend to Woodhull. They hit upon a Setauket man named Austin Roe, later known as Number 724. One historian has called Roe "The New York Paul Revere." His was a continually risky job, riding over enemy territory, and he was liable at any time to be stopped and searched.

The last link in the chain was Caleb Brewster, who had been a whaleboat privateersman before the war. His job was to see that the messages were taken safely across the Sound, ferrying them to the Connecticut shore where John Bolton's dragoons were waiting to take them to Washington.

The system worked like this: Austin Roe would drop in at the coffee house where Culper Jr. was apt to be found talking to some British officers, with whom he was on the best of terms.

After a few minutes, Culper Jr. would drift out of the coffee house and Roe would follow him. In some safe place Culper Jr. would give Roe his message, which the latter would conceal, and off he went on horseback, on his long, dangerous ride to Setauket, through enemy country.

Roe did not attempt to go near Culper Sr. He buried his message in a box in a field. There Culper Sr. retrieved it and sent it on to Brewster who was to get it across the Sound. There were half a dozen places where Brewster might land his boat. Some distance away, but where Brewster could see it with high-powered glasses, was a clothesline. The number of handkerchiefs, from one to six, hanging on the line showed which landing place was being used. At the proper landing place Culper Sr. looked for a boat with a black petticoat hanging over the side, and turned the message over to Brewster.

There was still one unsolved problem. To one living in enemy territory, there was constant danger of being caught and searched. How were the messages to be sent so they would be undetected?

Here help came from an unexpected source. John Jay had a brother James who was living in England. This brother had amused himself by inventing an invisible ink, or "stain," as he called it. There was one vial of stain with which the letter was written on very white paper. When a second vial of stain was brushed over the letter, the message was revealed. It was, James Jay said, with this invisible ink that he had been able to send America the first word of the determination of the British ministry to reduce the Colonies to unconditional submission.

At first, Washington was startled because the Culpers wrote their messages on blank sheets of paper. Anyone would realize that a message must be hidden. He suggested that they write camouflage letters, addressed to some well-known Tory, dealing with family or business matters, and with their real message concealed between the lines. Or, sometimes, they might put their hidden message on the blank pages of a pamphlet or book. Or, still another idea—for Washington was full of suggestions for the practical work of spies—the message might be folded in a particular manner so he would be able to identify it and look for the invisible writing.

Of course, even with all these precautions, things did not always go smoothly. On one occasion, Culper Jr. was in such a hurry to deliver an urgent piece of intelligence to Washington that he sent his cousin, James Townsend, instead of waiting for his regular messenger, Austin Roe. James was not accustomed to spy activities and he became confused. Which house was he supposed to go to? He wasn't sure. He picked one and knocked at the door. The people of the house, if he could judge by their talk, were Tories. So he, too, talked like a Tory.

Then, to his embarrassment and surprise, they took him prisoner. They were part of the American army. They searched his pockets and found a folded paper containing a poem called "The Lady's Dress."

This effusion was sent on to Washington, who saw that the poem had been folded into sixteenths. It was a stain letter. But what was he to do about poor James Townsend? If the army were asked to release the prisoner, the real activities of Robert Townsend would be suspected. Any casual comment dropped about him might end his usefulness forever. It was some time before Washington was able to devise a way of releasing James Townsend safely.

But almost always the message written in invisible ink, and carried from link to link of the spy chain, reached its destination safely. Washington was kept constantly informed of what the British were doing in New York. At one time, indeed, Culper was even able to warn Washington that there was a British spy in his own camp.

Townsend sent Washington word of the number of British troops, where they were stationed, what provisions they had and where the supplies came from. Carpenters were arriving. That meant the building of boats and the erection of winter quarters. The British were raiding American farms for supplies, not caring whether their victims were Whigs or Tories. This was enraging the Tories, who expected special treatment. A piece of good news for Washington.

Then, one day, Townsend came across a piece of intelligence of great urgency. Some American traitor in high place had betrayed the approach of the French fleet under Rochambeau, which was expected at Newport. A British admiral with eleven ships was already on the way to Rhode Island. The British expected an easy victory because the French fleet consisted only of "seven sail."

The destruction of the French fleet would have been a major disaster to the American cause. But Townsend's message arrived at headquarters in time. Immediately Washington let "intelligence" leak through to the British that he planned to attack New York. The British hastily withdrew their forces from Newport to New York and the French arrived safely.

For this one message alone the Culper service would have been invaluable. But there were dozens before that and the greatest was yet to come.

In the Townsend house at Oyster Bay the British officers gravitated around Robert's pretty sister Sarah. Her chief admirer was Colonel Simcoe, one of whose frequent visitors was young Major John André. André was one of those charming young men who are liked by everyone. Not even his political enemies ever seem to have disliked André himself. Good-looking, polished and witty in manner, gentle but brave, adventurous, he was, at twenty-nine, not only a major in the British army but head of General Howe's spy ring in New York. No one among the Americans and few among the British had any inkling of this fact.

One day, Sarah Townsend noticed in surprise that a man slipped into the house and hid a letter in a cupboard in the kitchen. When he had gone, Sarah looked for the letter and saw that it was addressed to Mr. John Anderson. Instead of opening it or taking it, the quick-witted girl put it back where she had found it and then set herself to watch.

Some time later her patience was rewarded. Major André, gay and full of fun as usual, dropped in to call. Through the open kitchen door he saw a bowl of fresh hot doughnuts. Laughingly, he went into the kitchen and helped himself to a handful of the hot doughnuts. He also swiftly helped himself to Mr. John Anderson's letter. After the usual exchange of compliments and banter, the young major went upstairs to the room occupied by his friend, Colonel Simcoe.

Sarah, moving softly and watchful of creaking boards, crept close to the door. She listened, holding her breath. There were only two words she could distinguish in that whispered conversation, but she heard them over and over—the words *West Point*.

At once, Sarah wrote a note to her brother. Never at a loss for a willing messenger from among her British admirers, she asked an infatuated young captain to find a horse and rider to go to her brother's store in New York. She needed a certain

66

kind of tea for her party next day.

That night, Townsend had his sister's message and, twenty-four hours later, Major Tallmadge was reading a strange note about Major John André who received letters addressed to John Anderson and had a deep interest in West Point.

A trivial message it must have seemed, but if Major Tallmadge had failed to receive it, John André might have reached Benedict Arnold and West Point might have been delivered into the hands of the British. It is not impossible that the outcome of the Revolution rested, at least in part, on the delivery of that message from Culper.

The name John Anderson was not completely unknown to Major Tallmadge. Only a few days before, he had received a letter from West Point saying: "If Mr. John Anderson, a person I expect from New York, should come to your quarters, I have to request that you will give him some escort of two horse to bring him on his way to this place, and send an express to me that I may meet him." It was signed by Benedict Arnold, the general in command at West Point.

As it happened, Major Tallmadge was away from his post on duty for several days. While he was gone a spy was captured and brought in. Tallmadge was told about it. The spy, he was told, had been sent, with a strong guard, to General Arnold. The man's name was John Anderson.

Anderson! The pieces of the puzzle fell together. Now Tallmadge understood both Arnold's orders and that strange little note from Culper. But he dared not use Culper's warning as evidence. He had sworn never to betray the spy's identity.

However, he could at least prevent Anderson from reaching Benedict Arnold, and he sent mounted men in all haste to bring him back.

This discovery of Arnold's treachery was not an overwhelming shock to Tallmadge. "With Arnold's character," he wrote, "I became acquainted while I was a member of Yale College and he residing at New Haven, and I well remember that I was impressed with the belief that he was not a man of integrity."

The story of Benedict Arnold's treason in all its ugliness is well known to everyone. Born into a distinguished family—one of his great-grandfathers had been three times governor of Rhode Island—he ran away from home at fifteen.

His early service during the Revolution, in which he rose from captain to brigadier-general, deservedly made him famous. But while his professional record was brilliant his private conduct was causing much discussion. Drinking, gambling, heavy spending. In Philadelphia, his actions finally led to four charges being brought against him and he had considerable difficulty in clearing himself.

About this time he married Margaret Shippen and began to lay plans for his treason, which was a straight business bargain: so much information for so much cash. He informed the British of the approach of the French fleet, under Rochambeau, as a sign of good faith. This act of treachery had been defeated by Culper Jr. Arnold also tried to persuade both General Washington and the young French general Lafayette to give him the names of their New York spies. Fortunately, both men refused to do so, not because they distrusted Arnold but because they were determined to keep faith with their men.

For months, Arnold had plotted to get the command at West Point. To his dismay, Washington, instead, offered him the post of honor, command of the left wing of the whole Continental army. Arnold awkwardly refused. His health made it impossible for him to be active in the field, he declared. Washington was considerably surprised, but he gave him the West Point command.

Arnold was delighted. So was his wife Peggy, who was a great friend of André.

Arnold set to work turning his American property into cash and transferring it to London. He would also have the nice lump sum that Clinton had offered him—20,000 pounds in exchange for West Point. He sold what government supplies he could get his hands on, too, for cash. Then he scattered his troops far and wide so as to weaken the fort and then waited for "Mr. Anderson" to arrive and close the bargain.

Small wonder that an American lieutenant-colonel had written of him three years earlier: "Money is this man's god and to get enough of it he would sacrifice his country."

In New York, young André and his fire-eating friend Simcoe had made stirring plans. Simcoe wanted to capture Washington. Then the correspondence with Arnold decided them on the capture of West Point. André's first attempt to meet Arnold was frustrated when gunboats opened fire on the ship he was in and he had to return to New York.

The second time was successful. Arnold ordered two reluctant men to slip out in a rowboat with muffled oars to the man-of-war which carried Mr. Anderson. The young man was taken to the place where the American general hid in a grove of fir trees.

"Mr. Anderson," one of these boatmen said later in his testimony, "from his youthful appearance and the softness of his manners, did not seem to me to be qualified for a business of such moment."

The two men conferred so long that morning came and

the sky was so light that Mr. Anderson could not return to his ship. Then it was attacked and had to leave, while the young man stared after it, white-faced. With that ship went his safety.

After the conference, André set out for New York. This time he had to go by land. He had discarded his uniform and wore a blue great-coat. He carried with him notes on the West Point defenses. He also carried a pass from General Arnold.

When he came near Tarrytown he ran into a party of men guarding the road. What happened to the usually alert and quick-witted André? The chances are that his mind was dulled from many successive and anxious nights almost without sleep.

"Gentlemen," he said, "I hope you belong to our party. The 'lower party.' I am a British officer."

When he learned that he had encountered the wrong party, he panicked and pulled out General Arnold's pass. Then the fat was in the fire. They searched his clothes. When they tried to remove his boots, he protested. Inside his stockings they found the hidden papers.

"This is a spy."

They took him to Tallmadge's headquarters and, in the major's absence, sent him on to General Arnold.

How his heart must have leaped with relief at that order! How it must have sunk with sick foreboding when Tallmadge sent guards to bring him back!

The rest of the story is familiar. Benedict Arnold escaped from West Point a bare half-hour before Washington arrived. The British made Arnold a brigadier-general and later he attempted to persuade other American officers—Tallmadge among them!—to join him. The British received the informer but they neither liked nor trusted him. As for the Americans,

Culper Jr. summed up their attitude: "His name will stink to eternity."

Major André was given a military trial. Fourteen officers, including the French general Lafayette, heard the evidence. There was no possible doubt of André's guilt. He was sentenced to death, although, "Had he been tried by a court of ladies," Tallmadge remarked, "I am confident they would have acquitted him."

Washington himself would have released André if he could have done so. Three times he informed the British general Clinton that he would let André go if Clinton would only return Arnold.

But on October 2, 1780, young John André was hanged.

"All I request of you gentlemen," he said, as he mounted the cart and a noose from a rope over the branch of a tree was dropped around his neck, "is that you will witness to the world that I die like a brave man."

The cart was drawn away and he dropped.

One of those who most grieved for André was Culper Jr. who was, perhaps, most responsible for his capture. Several times on visiting his father's house, Raynall Hall, he had met the engaging young British officer and he liked him. But through André's correspondence with Arnold the identity of several of Washington's spies in New York had been discovered and they were promptly arrested by the British. For some time after Arnold's treachery became known, conditions in New York were more perilous than ever for Culper.

With the end of the war, Major Tallmadge built a beautiful home in the lovely village of Litchfield, Connecticut, and served for many years in Congress.

Brewster, who had run the ferry service across the Sound

for the spy ring, rose to be a colonel and later was granted a pension by Congress for gallantry in action. He served as skipper of a revenue cutter.

Culper Sr., Abraham Woodhull, was for more than ten years a judge in Suffolk County.

But Culper Jr., Robert Townsend, required no public office or public recognition. When the war was over he returned to Raynall Hall, his family home in Oyster Bay, now forever free from British officers. But his work for his country was not ended.

All during the war he had lived among the British as a Tory sympathizer. He knew better than any living man those who had been loyal to their country and those who had not. And Alexander Hamilton, the only man except Washington who ever transcribed his "stain" letters, knew his handwriting well. So, in the years of adjustment many letters reached Hamilton that told the background of this man and that, or made suggestions and offered opinions which were accepted and followed without question.

Culper, anonymous during the war, remained anonymous in peace, but his influence remained potent for the integrity and welfare of his country.

THE CIVIL WAR

ROSE O'NEAL GREENHOW, PERSUASIVE WOMAN

*T*HE CIVIL WAR, unlike the Revolution, was a clash between people of the same country, the same traditions, the same history. It was a family clash and, like most family disputes, more bitter than clashes with outsiders. Here friend fought friend and brother sided against brother.

Washington, D.C., was a hotbed of conflicting loyalties. It was the seat of the Federal government but it was still, as it had always been, more Southern than Northern in its loyalty. Clashing interests, open hostilities, hidden sympathies existed not only in Congress but in the government departments and in the army itself. No one could be sure to which side old friends and neighbors were secretly committed.

In a brick house at 13th and I Streets, not far from the White House, lived a charming widow, Mrs. Rose O'Neal Greenhow, "a woman of almost irresistible seductive power," a contemporary described her. The two-story and basement house, with its parlor elevated several feet above the ground, was a center of Washington social life. It was a far step from the boarding house, run by her aunt, Mrs. Hill, in the Old Capitol Building, where Rose had first stayed in Washington, when she had been sent there as a young girl by her family.

Although she was related to great southern families, the Lees and the Randolphs and the Calverts, Rose had been born of poor parents and lived in a country district in Maryland as a child. She was a pretty girl, with shining black hair, dark eyes, olive skin and full red lips. "The wild Rose," she was called as a girl. Irresistibly attractive, she was also immensely ambitious and, perhaps because of her modest bringing up, hungry for social position, prestige and power.

During her stay at the Congressional boarding house of her aunt, she met and came to know well, and probably to be deeply influenced by, the fiery John Calhoun of South Carolina, who was always ready to talk about the problems of the South and to defend the institution of slavery, which was becoming a burning issue.

"I am a Southern woman," Rose wrote later, "born with revolutionary blood in my veins, and my first crude ideas on State and Federal matters received consistency from the best and wisest men of their country."

In spite of her exceptional good looks and her charm, Rose did not marry until she was 26. She was ambitious socially and she knew what she wanted. She married a scholarly man, Dr. Greenhow, 17 years older than she, established, with a delightful home and a position in the State Department where he served as an interpreter.

But if her husband's position was good, she intended to make it better. She set to work to build a solid and influential social life, cultivating men in high position, Cabinet members, army officers, even minor government clerks, anyone who was able to do favors. Then she became what today would be called a "five percenter." She arranged to get jobs for people, to do them favors. She even managed to get promotion for army officers. All for pay, of course.

Later, when her correspondence was seized, the government was astounded and appalled by the wide extent of her influence.

At the same time, she found another way to make money, acting as a spy for the British while they were still active in the Southwest. Jessie Benton, who married the explorer Frémont, declared that she had been forced to translate their messages herself rather than send them to Greenhow because "his wife was in the pay of the British legation as a spy and our private information reached them through her."

Rose's husband died when she was thirty-seven, leaving her with four children. The "white-hot wild" widow, as she was called, now really got into her stride as a power not only in Washington society but in government circles as well. Her sister Ellen had married Dolly Madison's nephew, James Madison Cutts, and her niece, Susan Cutts, married Senator Stephen A. Douglas. Everyone was sure that Douglas would become President of the United States.

Meanwhile, of course, there was James Buchanan, the present incumbent, so frequent a caller at the brick house that Mrs. Greenhow was called "the Queen of the Administration." Small wonder that she was regarded as "the most persuasive woman ever known in Washington."

Then, to her great dismay, instead of Douglas, the unknown giant, Abraham Lincoln, moved into the White House. But Mrs. Greenhow was not easily defeated. The President himself might be out of reach of her blandishments, but there were the Cabinet officers and other men in high places. She cultivated Lincoln's Secretary of State, Mr. Seward. She entertained army officers and even minor government clerks more assiduously than ever.

Then, one day, Thomas Jordan, a lieutenant in the army who intended to go over to the Southern side, decided to create a spy ring in Washington. Who was better equipped for the work than Mrs. Greenhow? She had a wide range of acquaintances, her influence reached into most of the government departments, her sympathies were with the South, her social position set her above suspicion. Besides all this, she was bold, daring, filled with vitality and a zest for adventure.

Rose Greenhow accepted. "I employed every capacity with which God has endowed me, and the result was far more successful than my hopes could have flattered me to expect."

She began to build a spy ring, using government clerks, young girls, older society women, a banker, a dentist—the list seems endless. But, most important, she obtained information of vital importance from Union army officers and from members of Lincoln's own cabinet.

"I might almost be said to have assisted at Lincoln's cabinet councils, from the facilities I enjoyed, having *verbatim* reports of them."

The weakness of Rose Greenhow's spy system lay partly in the very zest and thrill with which she approached her work. She could move through Washington, she related with obvious enjoyment, "as the Indian savage in the trackless forest, with an enemy behind every bush." It lay partly in the amateurish methods she used. Her messages were easily detected and easily deciphered.

Union officers called at the brick house and basked in the smiles of the entrancing widow. They found themselves telling her all sorts of unexpected things, because she was so interested, such a good listener. They told her of troop movements, of new weapons. They even took her to see fortifications.

She sent her first message in July and she must have enjoyed the romantic trappings of disguise and mystery. A young girl dressed as a market girl. A message wrapped in silk rolled into a knot of hair. The girl set off in a market wagon and, when she had crossed the lines, changed to a riding habit and rode horseback to Fairfax Court House, which was General Bonham's headquarters. Here she let down her hair and removed the silk-wrapped message. General Bonham read that there was to be a big Federal advance about the middle of July.

Mrs. Greenhow was now in her stride. Her spy ring was working efficiently. She kept messages flying to the Southern generals on troop movements and Cabinet discussions. An obliging officer not only showed her the capital's fortifications but provided her with a full set of blueprints.

Then she made her greatest *coup*. She learned from a Union officer that McDowell had been ordered to advance on Manassas. She had "received a copy of the orders to McDowell." This situation seems completely incredible today, but it is evidence of the far-flung influence of this amazing woman.

After showing the range of her spy ring, into the very heart of the Union government, she called on a former clerk in the Department of the Interior to carry a code message:

"Order issued for McDowell to move on Manassas tonight."

Back came Captain Jordan's reply: "Let them come. We are ready for them."

And so they were. As a result of Rose Greenhow's timely warning, General Beauregard was able to assemble his scattered troops in time to meet McDowell at Manassas and then to win, with General Johnson, the first battle of Bull Run.

Never, perhaps, has there been any battle as strange as that of Bull Run. The people of Washington streamed out to watch

79

it as they might have watched a circus, equipped with opera glasses and picnic baskets. When it was over, the North had suffered a major defeat and the battlefield was strewn with the dead and the dying. The horrified picnickers crept home.

But in the brick house on 13th Street there was jubilation, and another message came from Captain Jordan: "Our President and our General direct me to thank you. The Confederacy owes you a debt."

Mrs. Greenhow was exultant. But meantime the Union authorities became aware of the extent of the valuable information that was reaching the Confederates. There was still no organized government spy service. That was not to come for many years. But the government departments and some of the generals, hastily and belatedly, were beginning to set up their own personal networks.

Controls began to tighten. People who crossed the lines too frequently were watched. And then Mrs. Greenhow blundered. A message for Captain Jordan was seized and the code was broken without difficulty. Mrs. Greenhow, whose luck had run out, gave another message to a man who proved to be a Union spy. From that time on, suspicions against her mounted steadily. Her house was secretly watched. The people who visited her began to arouse considerable interest.

One stormy night, three men watching a lighted window in her living room saw a tall and handsome captain of infantry, who was in charge of one of the stations of the provost-marshal, arrive at the brick house. One of the watchers, standing precariously on the shoulders of the other two, watched the conversation he could not hear, saw the two bend, absorbed, over a map.

Next morning, the traitor-captain was arrested. There was

no longer any doubt of Mrs. Greenhow's guilt. She was a Confederate spy. From that time on, she made no move unobserved. She was followed, wherever she went.

Possibly, she did not notice the men who shadowed her, but others did. While she was strolling along the street one day a friend passed her.

"Several men are watching you," the friend whispered, and went on.

At once, Rose Greenhow put her cipher in her mouth and swallowed it. She continued her leisurely walk to her house. Another of her spies went by. This time it was Mrs. Greenhow who whispered.

"Watch from the corner. If they arrest me I'll raise my handkerchief."

A small man approached her. It was America's most famous detective, Alan Pinkerton. He arrested her and she stood quietly. But she touched her lips with her handkerchief.

Of course, it had been Pinkerton's hope to arrest her secretly and to use her house as a trap in which to ensnare other members of the spy ring. But those who were not warned as a result of her signal were warned by her small daughter who ran out of the house, screaming at the top of her lungs, "Mother's been arrested! Mother's been arrested!" in order to keep away any unsuspecting member of the spy network.

Imprisoning Rose Greenhow proved to be a formidable task. She had all her wits about her and she was far from being defeated. The first plan was merely to keep her in house arrest, treating her "as honorably and courteously as possible."

They searched the house and found a number of incriminating papers, concerned not only with her work as a spy but involving her in a number of "deals" before the war. The most disturbing factor was the discovery that Rose Greenhow had been involved with so many people in high positions.

Careful as the authorities were to guard Mrs. Greenhow, they discovered that she was still slipping messages out under their very noses to the South. This happened not once but time after time.

At length, it appeared that house arrest was not practicable with this alert woman. So she was taken to the Old Capitol, once her aunt's boarding house where Rose had spent part of her girlhood, but now a prison.

Strange it may seem to us now that there was no thought that this spy should be shot, though such an end is almost automatic today. But that compassionate man, Lincoln, whom she so hated, could not bear to impose a death sentence.

In the Old Capitol Prison Mrs. Greenhow at once began to make her presence felt. A woman of her high social position in such a place! She proceeded to object to everything: to the room, to the food, to the guards, even to the other prisoners. And while she was creating all this uproar, she still managed to send out messages and intelligence gleaned from what she saw from her windows and heard from other prisoners! Sealed in a glass cage, she would probably have succeeded in slipping out intelligence to the enemy.

Still, no more severe penalty was exacted of her. Instead, she was released and sent across the lines to the Confederacy, with the order that she was not to return until the war was over.

In the South, she was welcomed with open arms. Jefferson Davis called on her to say: "But for you, there would have been no Bull Run."

For years, she had been living an active and exciting life.

Quiet was not for her. She was a born intriguer so, before long, well supplied with money from the Confederacy, she sailed for England. What the purpose of the trip and the money was, from the Confederate standpoint, is unknown. But Mrs. Greenhow had a spectacular personal success. She met Napoleon III in France and Queen Victoria in England. Some time before the end of that visit to England she became engaged to be married.

She also wrote a book about her war experiences, hoping to use it for propaganda purposes in England. And she seems also to have been heavily involved in financial deals.

Then, in August, 1864, she returned to America. No one knows the reason why she left her daughter and her fiancé in England to make the dangerous trip. The steamer was successful in running the blockade. It had nearly reached Wilmington when it ran on a bar.

Mrs. Greenhow was in a panic. Arrest now meant a return to the Old Capitol Prison, probably for the duration of the war. She and several other Confederate agents demanded to be put ashore at once. They were sent off in a boat. Somehow, the little boat overturned. The other agents escaped but Rose Greenhow sank. The weight of the gold which she wore strapped around her waist under her dress carried her down and she was drowned.

Later, a Confederate soldier found the body, robbed it of its gold and pushed it back into the water. But when it was at last identified as that of Rose O'Neal Greenhow, who was responsible for the Confederate victory at Bull Run, he made full restitution.

She had lived fully and adventurously. She died, as she had lived, a victim to the gold she loved.

PINKERTON AND HIS MEN

A DETECTIVE agency was a new and strange idea in the days of the Civil War. No one was quite sure just what its functions were. Even today, readers of the most famous of all detective novels, *The Moonstone* by Wilkie Collins, are puzzled to find that, in the middle of the nineteenth century, a detective attached to the police could be hired by a private person.

The first detective in Chicago was a man named Alan Pinkerton, middle-aged, a short, rather plump man, with a beard and a nondescript appearance. A man who could pass in a crowd unnoticed, unless one saw the keenly observant eyes.

Born in 1819 in Scotland, where his father, a Glasgow police sergeant, had died of injuries in a workmen's riot, Pinkerton came to Illinois where he set up business in a cooper's shop. From the beginning, he hated the idea of enslaving human beings and his shop became a part of the Underground Railway, which helped escaping slaves on their dangerous way to freedom.

It was in 1850 that Pinkerton became Chicago's first and only detective. Even the police force was brand-new. Then, with a lawyer friend, he opened the first successful private detective agency in the United States. Before long, he began to collect data on criminal activities, and in time and for many years to come he had the most complete file of criminal records in the United States.

Pinkerton found his profession a fascinating but exacting one. He was a prodigious worker, more often than not on the job from early morning until midnight. A sound judge of men, he began to collect around him assistants who were able, courageous and intelligent, qualities that were essential in a day when they had to rely only on their own efforts and had none of the scientific aids of modern criminal investigation.

Because of the competent work Pinkerton was doing, rumors soon reached far beyond Chicago and he was called on by the Department of the Treasury in Washington, while Franklin Pierce was President, to make some investigations for them. He also built a reputation for his detective work for railway and express companies. Eventually, his local agency became the National Detective Agency.

All this time, however, he continued to give what assistance he could to the Abolitionists. His home was "besieged by numbers of prayerful Negroes seeking his aid in behalf of some trembling and hunted fugitive."

Then Abraham Lincoln was elected President and bitterness between the pro- and anti-slavery forces intensified. Pinkerton's finest operative, and perhaps the greatest spy of the Civil War, was a man named Timothy Webster. Pinkerton had sent Webster to Baltimore, in January, 1861, to look into a rumor that traffic on the Philadelphia, Wilmington & Baltimore Railroad, then an essential link between New York and Washington, was to be disrupted.

In the course of his investigation, Webster picked up a hint that there was a plot afoot to murder Lincoln as he passed through Baltimore on his way to Washington for the Inauguration. At once, Webster passed on the warning to Pinkerton, who took immediate action. Lincoln was notified, the timing of the trip to Washington was altered and the President-elect was smuggled through Baltimore twelve hours earlier than had been expected.

There was considerable mockery over this "baseless rumor" at the time. Even Lincoln was amused by it. But eventually Webster's warning was proved, like all the intelligence collected by that remarkable man, to be correct. His information undoubtedly saved the President's life.

During his work for the railroads, Alan Pinkerton had come to the attention of the president of the eastern division of the Ohio & Mississippi Railroad, George B. McClellan. When McClellan went to Washington as a general, he hired Pinkerton to go with him as his personal spy. Then he extended his plan and wanted the detective to build up and manage a secret service bureau.

Pinkerton promptly agreed and, for his war work, used the alias of Major E. J. Allen. With him he took his best men, Timothy Webster and Pryce Lewis, as well as other operatives.

The first major assignment given Pinkerton by McClellan was to send men South to find out the strength of the Confederate forces. Pinkerton himself went as far as Jackson, Mississippi. Pryce Lewis went to Charleston, and Webster went to Baltimore. As a result of the intelligence gathered by these men, McClellan's campaign was successful in holding West Virginia in the Union.

One of Pinkerton's constant preoccupations was to find ways of protecting his agents and providing them with a suitable "cover" to insure their safety. In the long run, of course, each man's safety depended mainly upon his ability to keep his head in an emergency.

Pryce Lewis was a young man under thirty, with a pink, bewhiskered face and a noticeable English accent, as he was British born. After studying the man's personality, Pinkerton decided to send him South as an English nobleman. He picked another of his operatives, Sam Bridgman, to go along as Pryce's servant. Pryce Lewis was provided with the proper wardrobe, with fine wines and cigars, and a smart carriage, the harness mounted with silver—Pinkerton did not stick at expense if the details were important to the whole picture—and off they went.

Lewis carried with him forged letters of introduction to leading citizens and Sam, who called him "my lord" when anyone was around, was to make friends among the hotel keepers, farmers, anyone he could find, and pick up information.

Pinkerton's men were well trained, so they rarely missed an opportunity to gather intelligence. One day, for instance, the smart, glittering carriage drew up before a farmhouse. It was lunch time and the two spies were hungry. The farmer and his wife, dazzled by the silver-mounted harness, the elegant carriage, the gracious manners of the man addressed as "my lord," welcomed them in. They wanted to hear about England and brilliant society. The polite nobleman wanted to hear about a farmer's life.

The farmer said that he had ten sons, all in the Confederate army. Lewis prodded gently. Before the lunch was over he had learned where each son was stationed, in what company, who the Commander was, how many troops he had and where they were liable to be sent next. He had a nice budget of news to forward to Pinkerton that night.

Sooner or later, of course, even the most distinguished noble-man was bound to be stopped and asked to show a pass. This Pinkerton had been unable to provide, but Pryce Lewis was not at a loss. He was taken to Colonel George Patton, grand-father of General George Patton who distinguished himself in World War Two. Patton was pleased with this charming English visitor and not only gave him a pass but politely took him to inspect the fortifications.

Once Lewis went to Charleston where he put up at the best hotel. When it came to signing the register he hesitated for a moment and then scrawled his name. The effect on the people who saw this was that he was a great man traveling incognito.

In Charleston, Lewis began to run into trouble. He was the only man in the hotel who was not in uniform. English or not, this seemed suspicious. People speculated about this suave stranger. Was he what he pretended to be? To make it worse, Lewis discovered that his "servant," Sam Bridgman, had an unexpected weakness, one that is fatal for a spy. Now and then, he would get drunk, and when he was drunk he not only was indiscreet, he even went so far as to insult the Southerners.

General Henry A. Wise was not friendly to the Englishman who was not in uniform. He refused Lewis's request to see the Natural Bridge and other wonders, which Lewis told him he had come far to enjoy. Then, Lewis said haughtily, he would apply to the British Consul in Richmond. That, General Wise replied, was up to him.

Having made his bluff, Lewis was stuck with it. He had to write to the British Consul, who, of course, would inform the Confederates that this English nobleman was an imposter. So, before there could be any reply, Lewis must collect all the

intelligence he could and escape back North. Otherwise—
court martial and death as a spy.

No one would have guessed that Lewis was perturbed. With
the material provided for him by the painstaking Pinkerton,
he spun long tales of his military service in the Crimea. He
passed around the fine cigars and wine that had been furnished
him. The young officers found him delightful. They gathered
around, drinking his wine, and they talked and talked as their
tongues loosened. They took Lewis to see their camps and
showed him everything.

But time was running out. The British Consul's reply might
come any day. Sam's weakness for drink might betray them
even before that. Pryce Lewis had valuable intelligence and the
time had come to get out. And fast.

He didn't need a pass to go to Richmond. He and Sam
started for home. On the way they saw troops in the gray of
the Confederate uniform massing. When Lewis stopped for
the night, the obliging host learned that he wanted to go to
Richmond, introduced the distinguished stranger to the Com-
mandant in charge of the Southern troops, who not only told
him the best way to travel but arranged for him to give an
informal talk to his men that night. Which Lewis did! A spy
finds himself called upon to do the most unexpected things.

Of course, Lewis had no desire to go to Richmond where
the British Consul had probably already been alerted that he
was an impostor. Instead, he and Bridgman set off secretly for
Kentucky, traveling at top speed. And then in the distance
they saw the Stars and Stripes. They had made it!

Lewis reported to Pinkerton. He'd been gone only nineteen
days, and he declared that he had aged nineteen years. But he
brought back valuable intelligence. Because of what he had

learned, General Wise was forced to retreat from Charleston and General Cox marched in.

Meanwhile, Alan Pinkerton was working with his usual thoroughness and great capacity for detail. He began to check on the government departments, the army personnel, the highways and byways of Washington. He discovered to his dismay that Washington was filled with people who were hostile to the Union. There was not a government department free of informers for the enemy, no group of people that did not contain traitors.

The extent of Pinkerton's activities became known to Thomas A. Scott, Assistant-Secretary of War, who sent for him. There was a certain beautiful woman of high social position who had aroused suspicion. He asked Pinkerton to investigate. This was Mrs. Rose O'Neal Greenhow, who had already been responsible for the Federal defeat at Bull Run, though that was not known then.

Pinkerton ordered that everyone coming to or going from the brick house on 13th Street was to be watched. He took two men with him, one of them Pryce Lewis, who had returned from his dangerous tour of the South as an English lord. The house was dark, no sign that anyone was there.

Then a "storm broke with terrible violence." The men were drenched to the skin and ran for shelter. "On my return," Pinkerton reported, "the blinds were still down but there were lights on the parlor floor."

He was a small man and the two operatives were much bigger. Pinkerton took off his shoes and stood on their shoulders. Noiselessly he raised a window and turned a blind so he could see.

Then footsteps approached the house. Again the three silent watchers broke for cover. When the visitor had entered the house they returned to the window where they watched the charming widow examine a map with her victim.

When the traitor left the house, Pinkerton followed him through the downpour, not daring to stop to put on his shoes. So far as he could tell, the captain was unaware that he was being followed. He entered a building. Immediately four armed soldiers came out and stood with fixed bayonets pointed at Pinkerton's heart. The building the captain had entered was a station of the provost-marshal.

Pinkerton was dragged inside. What did he mean, the captain demanded, by following him? He had simply been lost in the rain, the detective replied. Looking at the man, soaking wet, without shoes, the captain grew more furious.

"What is your name?"

"E. J. Allen."

"What is your business?"

"I have nothing further to say. I decline to answer any more questions."

"Very well, sir." The captain snapped at one of his men: "Take this man to the guardhouse but allow no one to converse with him. We shall attend to his case in the morning."

Pinkerton was taken to a cell in which a couple of Secessionists were being held under arrest. Late that night he held a whispered conversation with his guard and urged him to carry a secret message to Assistant-Secretary Scott when he went off duty in the morning.

At six o'clock, the guard went to awaken the Assistant-Secretary of War, who summoned both the captain and his prisoner, E. J. Allen, to appear before him at his house.

Scott had a brief private interview with Pinkerton. Then he sent for the captain. What was the reason for this man's arrest? Allen had followed him in a very suspicious way, the captain said, when he was returning from a call on a friend.

"Captain," Scott asked, "did you last evening see anyone who is unfriendly to the government?"

"No."

"You may consider yourself under arrest."

Pinkerton at once instituted a search and found evidence that the captain had been furnishing intelligence to the enemy, and he was imprisoned. After a year in prison he died, and it seems likely that he committed suicide.

His arrest led also to the end of Rose Greenhow's activities as a spy in Washington.

Greatest of all Pinkerton's operatives was Timothy Webster, who was to assume the risky job of the double spy. He, like Pryce Lewis and Pinkerton himself, was British born. Starting as a machinist in Princeton, New Jersey, he became a police sergeant at the first world's fair, held at the Crystal Palace in New York. The superintendent of New York police who recommended him to Pinkerton—Webster was then thirty-five years old—said: "He is the bravest, coolest man, I think, that ever lived."

Unlike Pinkerton's, his was a memorable appearance. He was tall, good-looking, impressive. His manner, his dignity, his steady eyes gave him "an air of trust." People instinctively believed in him. "He practically mesmerized you into thinking he was whatever he decided to be," said one of his fellow operatives.

In other words, Webster's kind of disguise or cover was

the hardest of all, the sheer force of personality that imposed on others a complete acceptance of and belief in the particular character he chose to assume.

An all-round athlete, physically powerful, a crack shot, he was fearless but at the same time he took no unnecessary risks. His judgment was superb. Above all, he had an almost incredible capacity for grasping and improving every opportunity that arose to gather intelligence and to create a feeling of esteem that made men believe in him in the face of the strongest adverse evidence. Of him Pinkerton said: "No danger was too great, no trust too responsible."

Even before the Civil War broke out, Timothy Webster had learned to walk the tight rope of danger with ease and confidence. Hourly faced with the possibility of exposure and death, he seemed relaxed and casual in all his dealings. Sometimes, indeed, Webster played his part so well that he deceived even his own side and ran into danger from the Union forces. Once when he was in Pittsburgh on a job for Pinkerton, some Northern sympathizers believed him to be a Confederate spy.

"Lynch him!"

He stood backed against a wall, facing them alone. Then Pinkerton pushed his way through the blood-thirsty mob and stood beside him, gun drawn, waiting. He'd sent for help but would it arrive in time? In any case, Pinkerton would back his men to the death. And then, when it seemed that the two men could no longer hold back the mob, the Chief of Police arrived to disperse the angry crowd and save the beleaguered detectives.

It was Timothy Webster who, on that early trip to Baltimore to investigate the plot against the railroad, had unearthed the grimmer plot to murder President-elect Lincoln. Typical of

93

Webster's methods, he had acquired his information by becoming friends with some of the Maryland cavalry and joining the conspirators. Posing as an outspoken Secessionist, he made friends who later helped him to extend his acquaintance among the Confederate leaders.

Indeed, some of these men were to prove of use to him in the only other association he was to have with President Abraham Lincoln. Shortly after the Inauguration, a secret document had to be sent to the President and Pinkerton was asked to handle the matter. He called upon Timothy Webster, who sewed the papers inside his coat collar and his vest lining.

At this time it was difficult to get into Washington, but Webster managed to find a man with a wagon who would take him as far as Baltimore. There were other passengers in the wagon, one of them an Englishman. When they reached Baltimore, Webster encountered one of the men whom he had met on his earlier trip, one of those who had intended to murder Lincoln. The man hailed him as a friend and gave him a pass to Washington.

This greatly impressed the Englishman and he told Webster that he, too, was working for the South. In fact, he was the bearer of important letters to Southerners in Washington.

When the wagon stopped at lunch time, Webster looked around and spotted a man whose sympathies were with the North. A few quiet words. The Union man finished his lunch quickly and set off for Washington at a gallop. By the time the wagon rumbled up, an armed guard stopped it. Everyone was to be searched. The Englishman's papers were seized and both men were arrested.

Released secretly, Webster went at once to the White House. There Lincoln watched while he took off his coat and vest and ripped them open to remove the papers he had brought. Lincoln thanked him warmly. He also thanked him for the capture of the Englishman whose papers had proved to be of real importance.

After several visits to Baltimore, Webster had built a secure position as a Confederate sympathizer. Once, indeed, he and John Scully, another Pinkerton agent, had a daguerrotype picture made, showing them holding a huge Confederate flag between them. Webster may not have seemed to be busy on some of these trips, but he was making friends. One young Confederate officer would introduce him to another until he had a wide circle of acquaintances among army men in high position.

He talked little himself, but he inspired confidence and stimulated others to talk. Reserved by nature, he could appear to be the most genial and expansive of companions. And all the time his eyes and ears were alert. Without asking questions he was able to supply Pinkerton with exceedingly valuable intelligence. He found out the number of troops, their strength, their sources of supply.

Then he offered to take letters from the Southerners to their friends in Washington, a convenient and useful passport. The friends answered. A roster of the unsuspected enemies within Washington itself was rapidly being drawn up.

On these frequent visits to Maryland, Webster managed to bring to light some of the underground activities that were going on. Strongest of these underground organizations was the Knights of Liberty, which had a loose association with the Confederate army and was potentially dangerous. Before long, Webster had been invited to join the Knights of Liberty and he promptly did so. He was horrified to discover the size and power of the group. They had 6,000 stands of arms concealed in Baltimore. There were 10,000 men waiting to attack Washington from the North when the Confederate army attacked from the South.

After Webster's report was received, orders came from Washington that the Knights of Liberty must be destroyed. Pinkerton sent down more operatives whom Webster managed to get into the group as members. Federal troops were summoned. Arrangements moved as smoothly as clockwork. One night, a mass meeting of the Knights of Liberty was called. Webster stationed his own men as guards at the doors. At the agreed time he rose to make a speech. Out poured a flood of impassioned oratory. Then came the words: "The smoking ruins of the city of Washington."

That was the signal for which the Federal troops were waiting. At the cue, Pinkerton's men threw open the doors, the troops surrounded the Knights of Liberty, and the whole dangerous underground was destroyed, by one master stroke.

On another occasion, Webster had just come back from a trip to Washington and, as usual, he was surrounded by friends. He was passing on the news he had heard in the capital—carefully chosen so as to do no harm to the Northern side—when an angry man pushed his way into the center of the group.

"Gentlemen," he shouted, "this man comes among you as a spy."

There was a moment's shocked silence, then indignation. Timothy Webster a spy? Impossible!

If Webster's nerves tightened, if he was aware of shock, there was no sign of it. Alone, surrounded by enemies in enemy territory, he looked around him with serene dignity.

"I don't understand you. What do you mean?"

The Southerner turned to the group around Webster. "I saw him in Washington yesterday."

Of course, Webster agreed. He'd just been passing on some bits of news he had heard there.

The other sneered. "Did you tell them you talked with the Chief of the Secret Service?"

"You're a liar."

The hot-headed Southerner pulled out a knife. Webster stood with a pistol in his hand.

"I'd as soon accuse Jeff Davis of being a Yankee spy," one of the Secessionists declared.

Webster's accuser stormed off in a rage. After all, he had actually seen the man in conversation with the Secret Service Chief. But not long afterwards something happened that convinced him of Webster's innocence. He made a full apology and lined himself up as one of Webster's most enthusiastic admirers.

Pinkerton, alert to the importance of protecting his men as far as possible, was careful to see that their identity was unknown, even to his other operatives, unless for some reason they were to work together.

Webster had just made his first trip to Richmond and was returning home. By now he was well known in the South as an ardent Secessionist. In Baltimore, one of Pinkerton's own men arrested him as a Confederate spy and he was locked up in a cell. Pinkerton heard of this important arrest a few hours later. He was in a bad spot. If he let Webster stay in jail he would lose his best man. If he had him released, the Southerners would become suspicious.

So Pinkerton arranged to have an escape staged so as to be as dramatic—and convincing—as possible. Orders were given

97

to transfer the prisoner to Fort McHenry. After they got started, Webster "escaped" from the patrol wagon. There was much noisy shooting and a mock pursuit by soldiers who were careful not to see which way he went.

Webster, quick to improve any opportunity, fled straight to the house of some well-known Southern sympathizers, who were delighted to hide him. The story later got a great deal of publicity in a Baltimore paper. Timothy Webster's identity as a loyal Secessionist was fully established. Small wonder that Pinkerton said of him: "Webster's talent for sustaining a role of this kind amounted to positive genius; in a lifetime of detective experience I have never met one who could more readily adapt himself to circumstances."

And now, to get back to that trip to Richmond, which, for sheer daring and enterprise, was unequalled by any other spy activity on either side during the Civil War.

Webster knew that the best introduction he could carry to a strange city would be letters from friends. There were many of his acquaintance in Baltimore who were eager to communicate with family or friends farther South. A smuggler who carried passengers, mail and cargo across the Chesapeake Bay got him safely to Gloucester Point.

At Spotswood House in Richmond, Webster settled down. He delivered his letters, received grateful thanks and hospitality. He also increased his circle of friends. Most fortunate of all, he met the Confederate Secretary of War, Judah P. Benjamin, won his confidence, conferred with him and got a list of supplies of which the Southern War Department was sorely in need.

From that time, Timothy Webster skated on thin ice in his perilous role of double spy. From now on, the slightest slip meant death. And yet, apparently, Timothy Webster himself never made a single mistake. When disaster overtook him it was because of the carelessness and stupidity of his own colleagues.

But meanwhile, all was serene. Webster moved around Richmond as easily as if it were his own home. His friends eagerly took him on a tour of inspection of the city's earthworks, and showed him the batteries. They informed him that 12,000 Confederate rifles and some cannon had just arrived on an English ship which had evaded the blockade.

This was a familiar experience to the imperturbable Webster. After all, he had once been offered the rank of colonel in a Southern regiment. And he was the man who had drifted into Tennessee to look around, and had met a man at a bar who took him to a political rally. Here he met a Confederate officer who showed him around his camp. There he had met a general who told him about his troubles in getting supplies. With Webster one thing always led to another.

On his second trip to Richmond, Webster was ready to deliver some of the supplies requested by Secretary of War Benjamin. The Confederate Secretary was greatly impressed by this individual who could obtain items that were impossible for him to find. Actually, of course, they had been supplied with the permission and the assistance of the Federal government, in order to fortify Webster's position, though they included nothing that would be of major importance to the South's war effort.

In a hotel in Maryland the observant Webster noticed a man who was having a bad attack of nerves. The man confided in the sympathetic stranger. Doubtless Webster had already been pointed out to him as a distinguished Southern sympathizer. The nervous man said that he was Dr. Gurley. He was deserting the Union cause for the South and he was carrying important sealed dispatches for Secretary of War Benjamin. How was he to get them safely to Richmond?

Timothy Webster said he'd try to think of a way. This time his assistant was John Scoball, formerly a Mississippi slave, who had not only been freed but educated by a Scot who had owned him. Webster and Scoball held a secret conference. Then Webster sauntered back to the hotel.

Later, the timorous Dr. Gurley went out for a walk. Perhaps Webster had recommended fresh air and exercise for his nerves. When he returned he was almost hysterical. He had been set upon and robbed. His papers had been taken from him. He was ruined. How could he face Secretary Benjamin now?

"If you can remember the contents . . ." Webster suggested.

"But they were sealed! I don't know what they contained."

Webster sighed, apparently with sympathy, actually with relief. No danger that Benjamin would ever know about the dispatches, which were now being read by Pinkerton in Washington.

Strong as his position appeared, Webster realized as clearly as anyone that a single slip could be the end. So far, he had managed to wriggle out of tight spots by sheer boldness. When he got ready to leave Richmond this time a clerk named Jones in the War Department refused him a passport. Webster moved back and forth through the lines too often for his liking. What other person was going from South to North so regularly?

Webster's hesitation was brief. He did not lose his temper. Then, he said coolly, he'd apply to the Secretary of War himself. He did so. Benjamin promptly issued his passport.

Like a man with a charmed life, Webster made his reports to Pinkerton and went back to Richmond on his next trip. He crossed the Potomac in an open boat among whose passengers were a number of women and children. That night a storm came up and the little boat broke apart on a sand bar. Through the icy water Webster carried women and children to safety, making four trips in all. Then, his clothes soaking wet and freezing, he led them over a mile to a cabin where they would be sheltered. He himself spent the rest of the night lying on the ground. As a result of that night of heroic rescue, he developed an agonizing and crippling inflammatory rheumatism which never again left him.

But, being Webster, even out of that night he wrested a victory. In the dark and confusion one of the passengers lost a packet. Webster picked it up. As soon as he could do so, he examined it. He found a map of the country around Washington, information about the troops stationed there and a survey of the plans for the spring campaign.

Next day, the packet was on its way to Pinkerton, whose careful study of the government personnel paid off. The writing, he pointed out, was that of a clerk in the office of the provost-marshal in Washington. So another traitor was caught.

Meanwhile, Webster continued on his trip South. But the pain of the rheumatism was so unbearable that he had to stop for a few days in Fredericksburg before he could continue his journey.

When he returned to Washington, he was, as usual, well supplied with intelligence about Southern supply requirements and troop movements. Ill as he was, he waited only to collect the supplies he had promised to take South and he left again on his last trip to Richmond.

And then—there was silence. Week after week, Pinkerton waited in growing anxiety. Timothy Webster was not only the best operative he had ever known and a man performing invaluable service to his country—he was, in a way, a one-man army—but Pinkerton liked and valued him for himself. What could possibly have gone wrong?

At last, he could bear the suspense no longer. He must have news. He picked two of his most able men: Pryce Lewis, who had played the role of an English nobleman successfully in the South, and another operative, John Scully. They were good men but, for this particular job, they were probably the worst choice Pinkerton could have made. The great detective made an error of judgment of which Timothy Webster would never have been guilty. He selected men whom he had used in Washington to search the houses of suspected persons. As many of these had been sent South there was a strong chance that they might recognize Pinkerton's operatives.

To provide all three operatives with a safe cover, Pinkerton gave Lewis and Scully a letter to Webster. It introduced them as "friends of the South" and warned him that his old route back to Washington was no longer safe. The writer of the letter posed as a Confederate spy.

In Richmond, Pryce Lewis and John Scully inquired for Timothy Webster. They learned that he was at the Monumental Hotel where he had been staying for some weeks, unable to leave his bed because of crippling arthritis. Now this, after all, was the information that Pinkerton wanted: to be sure his best operative was alive and not in trouble with the Confederacy.

But Lewis and Scully seem to have lost their heads. They

promptly went to call on Webster who lay in bed, too crippled to move and in great pain. But, with his usual popularity, he was talking to a Southern friend. He received the two operatives with stiff formality and accepted the faked letter of introduction. Because of the presence of his visitor he was unable to give them any warning other than that conveyed by his manner. He was careful not to suggest that they call again.

Next day, however, Lewis and Scully again presented themselves in Webster's room. This time, a Confederate captain had come to cheer the invalid. Webster, unable to move, trapped by his own associates, watched helplessly.

Without suspicion, simply as a friendly reminder, the captain pointed out that neither Lewis nor Scully had as yet reported their presence in the town. They immediately went to do so and explained that Lewis was a visitor from England and Scully from Ireland.

Then, for the third time, they went back to Webster's room. They were shortly followed by a clerk who wanted to know from what parts of England and Ireland they came.

Webster knew then that they were under suspicion and that, by paying him three visits, they had inevitably thrown suspicion on him. What he did not know then was that a man in the office where they had reported their arrival in Richmond had recognized them as operatives who had searched his house in Washington.

Webster's position was far worse than theirs but his first instinct was to protect his associates as far as possible.

"Leave Richmond," he managed to say, almost soundlessly.

It was too late. When Lewis and Scully had closed the door of Webster's room behind them, they were arrested. After a trial they were sentenced to hang. Then they were released—

because John Scully made a full confession, naming Timothy Webster as the master spy in Richmond.

So crippled and wasted by illness that he could not move, the court martial of Webster was held beside his bed. He was sentenced to death.

There was consternation in Washington. Pinkerton, in a fury, appealed to Lincoln. That evening, the President called a special meeting of the Cabinet. It was decided that the Secretary of War would take up the matter with the Confederate authorities. He was to remind them that, whatever the provocation, the Union government had shown great leniency in dealing with Southern spies. Not a single one had been sentenced to death! Mrs. Greenhow and many others had only been imprisoned and usually sent back South after a certain length of time. Many of them had been freed without any penalty being imposed. But if Timothy Webster were to hang, the Union government would begin to exact a severe penalty in retaliation.

Lincoln himself, most gentle of men, seemed always to be pardoning Southern spies. There were a lot of people who did not approve of such softness. "You do not know how hard it is," he said, almost apologetically, "to let a human being die when you feel that a stroke of your pen will save him." Even on the day he himself was assassinated, one of his last acts was to free a condemned Southern spy.

But at Camp Lee there was a celebration. There were boos and shouts and laughter when Webster was taken out to be hanged. Except for his lameness, there was no sign of weakness until he was led past his waiting coffin. Then he shuddered.

The trap was sprung and the hangman's knot came loose. Webster fell heavily to the ground, with what agony one can guess. They had to carry him up this time, for he was too crippled to walk.

From under the cap pulled over his face came his voice, half smothered: "I suffer a double death."

It was Pinkerton who summed up Timothy Webster's life: "Brave, honest and intelligent, he entered the contest to perform his whole duty, and right nobly did he fulfill his pledge."

BELLE BOYD,
THE GAY OF HEART

"Seventeen and a saucebox," someone described her. Gay, friendly, fun-loving, she had great vitality and a strong sense of adventure. In fact, she imparted a quality of romantic adventure to everything she did. Not particularly good-looking, she made friends and created warm admirers and partisans wherever she went. Reckless and impulsive, warm-hearted and passionately devoted to the Southern cause, she ran headlong into the fierce clashes of the Civil War with a childlike faith that nothing could harm her and a laughing excitement that made every risk seem like a game.

At a time when most women, and particularly Southern women, were sheltered and chaperoned, she traveled alone, fearless and friendly, and she invariably met with protection and respect.

This was Belle Boyd, most famous of all the spies for the South.

She was born in Martinsburg, Virginia. Because she was incurably romantic and her imagination strongly colored her memories, as appears in her book about her war experiences, she recalled that childhood home as a most charming cottage.

Actually it must have been rather drab and poor. But Belle wasn't a girl to be sorry for herself. She was having too good a time living. As a child she was a tomboy, throwing herself into games, running or riding horseback.

At sixteen, having "grown up," she made her social début in Washington. But there was little time for a normal social life. Within a year the Civil War began and Martinsburg was so close to the Union lines that for the next four years it constantly fluctuated, now occupied by Union men, now occupied by Confederates. Something was always happening in the little town of Martinsburg, its streets filled with soldiers, and the war had scarcely begun before Belle had plunged into the thick of it.

No one was a stronger believer in the institution of slavery than Belle. The Negro cause of "race," she wrote later, "which prefers servitude to freedom . . . physically and morally an object of commiseration."

On the outbreak of the war, Belle's father was one of the first to volunteer, preferring, he said, to enlist in the ranks. With emotions at white heat and war talk filling the air, Belle found that the parties and usual routine of her days had become "too tame and monotonous to satisfy my temperament." She had to take part in what was going on.

It wasn't long before there were wounded Confederate soldiers in the little hospital, and Belle went to visit them. Her warm friendliness and her propensity to find every man in uniform a hero must have done them more good than the medicine of that day.

And then, on the Fourth of July, Union troops marched into Martinsburg and took possession. They behaved very badly. Some of the men got drunk, fired shots into houses, broke in and wrecked them.

"A party of soldiers broke into our house," Belle wrote. "They had brought the Stars and Stripes to put on the roof. My mother said, 'Men, every member of my household would die before that flag shall be raised over us.' "

According to Belle's own account, a drunken soldier insulted her mother and Belle promptly pulled out a pistol and shot him, killing him. As there is no official reference to this incident, however, it is probably one of her dramatic touches.

In any case, the Union soldiers threatened to burn down the house and Belle ran to their officer for help. That's the first account of the seventeen-year-old girl's invariable appeal to the chivalry of men, whether on her side or the enemy side. The officer not only withdrew his men before they could damage the Boyd house but he stationed sentries around it for Belle's protection.

In no time at all, Belle was acquainted with the Northern sentries and they were the best of friends, determined to protect this delightful girl at all costs. From them Belle turned her attention on the officers. One can imagine them sitting on the front porch on warm summer evenings, perhaps boasting a little, certainly talking more than they should to this attractive —but extremely alert—young lady.

The people of Martinsburg were highly critical of Miss Belle's friendly reception of the enemy. But she had her own ideas and she proceeded to follow them.

From her Northern admirers she began to pick up a good deal of information about the position and designs of the enemy. Whatever she learned she wrote down and sent to General J. E. B. Stuart. Without training or prompting from any outside force, she had already become a spy. But never was there such an amateur spy. Belle knew nothing of secret methods. She had no idea of covering her tracks.

She had been at this hazardous business—game, to her—only a short time when one of her messages was seized by the Yankees. Belle had used no code. She had not even thought of changing her handwriting. The message was identified almost at once as being in her writing, and she was taken to headquarters.

"They read the Article of War to me," she related.

They probably read the riot act to her as well. But one can imagine the scene: the official background, the officers looking stern, the girl wide-eyed and excited and interested. Of course, they let her go with a warning.

After the battle of Bull Run, a hospital for wounded Confederates was opened in the town of Front Royal and Belle "was installed one of the 'matrons.'" Here for nearly two months she worked hard as a nurse. Then her health broke under the strain and she had to go home to Martinsburg to recuperate.

By this time, word was being passed through the South of the activities of the beautiful spy, Mrs. Rose O'Neal Greenhow, who had played so large a part in the Southern victory at Bull Run. Particularly that story about the girl riding with a message hidden in a silken package in her hair. The glamour of that made a strong impression on Belle. What Rose Greenhow had done, Belle could do.

In October, her father's company was at Manassas and Belle went with her mother to visit him. There, she said, she acted as a courier between General Beauregard, General Jackson and their subordinates.

After returning to Martinsburg, Belle went riding one evening with two of her cousins. Her horse ran away and crossed the Union lines. Two Union officers saw her and politely offered to escort her back to safety. On her own side of the line she called to her cousins.

"Here are two prisoners," she said calmly.

The three youngsters proudly escorted their prisoners to headquarters and were greatly disappointed when they were released an hour later.

All that winter Martinsburg passed from the Confederates to the Union troops and back again. Something was always happening. And Belle was in the thick of whatever happened. Whether the troops in possession were Northern or Southern, they all liked the sprightly girl with her warm friendliness and her laughter. They congregated around her—and they talked. And off went Belle's reports.

By the following spring, the Union troops were again marching on Martinsburg. "I had gained some notoriety," Belle said, "so father sent me to Front Royal." A few days later, it, too, fell to the Union troops and Belle started home again.

She was arrested as a spy and taken to Baltimore for questioning. Was she daunted? Not Belle Boyd. Triumphantly she waved a Confederate flag over her head and laughed at her captors. They "imprisoned" her in a good hotel where she was treated with all possible courtesy and was even allowed to entertain her friends. A week later she was released and sent back home.

By this time, however, Belle's activities were beginning to seem more serious to the Union forces. When Belle reached Martinsburg she discovered that she not only could not leave the town but that she was to be under guard in her own house. The inactivity was more than she could bear. Belle was not a girl to sit placidly indoors watching life go on outside.

At length, she succeeded in getting a pass so she could go to Front Royal. She was planning to visit some relatives in Richmond. On her arrival she discovered that Union officers had taken over the house and her relatives had been forced to move into a small cottage on the grounds.

Belle decided that she would go on to Baltimore, so she wrote to General Sheilds to ask for a pass. To her surprise, the Union general came to see her himself. He exchanged banter with this young "enemy," but in doing so he gave away inadvertently some information about troop movements, which Belle was quick to note and remember. The general asked her permission to introduce some of his officers to this attractive and now famous Southern girl. The young officers were delighted. They brought her flowers, flattered her and, as usual, talked too much. How could they help it when her interest was so genuine?

General Sheilds, it appeared, was soon to leave. The night before his departure Belle learned, probably from one of the young officers, that he was to hold a council of war. The only suitable place for such a meeting would be in her aunt's drawing room.

"Immediately above this was a bedchamber, containing a closet, through the floor of which I observed a hole had been bored." So up the stairs Belle crept, as quietly as possible. She lay on the floor, her ear to the hole, and listened to the conversation.

It was one o'clock in the morning before the meeting broke up, the officers had gone to their quarters, and it was safe for her to leave the house. Back to the cottage she went, took down in cipher what she had heard. The use of a cipher indicates that Belle had learned a great deal since her first amateur approach to the dangerous job of spying.

Then, said Belle, "I went to the stables, saddled my horse, and galloped away in the direction of the mountain."

Some Confederate soldiers had obligingly provided her with passes so she was able to cross the sentry line and complete her fifteen-mile ride safely, over fields and marshes, in the dark.

At the Confederate headquarters she announced that she had "important intelligence," handed over her cipher message and started back. She made the return trip in two hours, once "running the blockade" of a sleeping sentry who awakened too late but managed to fire a shot after the flying figure.

Belle's next exploit came up when she decided to go to Winchester to do some shopping. "Lieutenant H.," as she referred to him, was a young Union officer who seems to have been dazzled by Belle's charms. She must have had an extraordinarily warm appeal to have continued to be so blindly trusted by Northern officers after she was known to be working for the Southern cause.

In any case, Lieutenant H. not only provided a pass, he offered to drive Belle, her cousin and her servant to Winchester. While Lieutenant H. was busy with official business, Belle carried on a transaction of her own. She met a Southern friend who gave her two packages of letters that must be sent through the lines to the Confederate army. One of them, he said, was of great importance, the other was trifling. A little note, which he handed her, was very important and it must be sent safely to General Jackson or to some other responsible officer.

Belle considered the best way to carry the documents. The important one she hid in her maid's clothing. The less important one she dropped in a basket she was carrying. She marked it, "Kindness of Lieutenant H." The small note she held carelessly in full view in her hand.

When Lieutenant H. met her, they started back. At the picket lines they were stopped by two detectives.

"We have orders to arrest you," they told Belle, "on suspicion of having letters."

They were taken to the headquarters of Colonel Beale. Belle was afraid of being searched, because of the importance of the documents she carried. To prevent it, she promptly reached into the basket and handed them her harmless package.

The colonel looked at it. "What! Kindness of Lieutenant H. What is the meaning of this?"

Poor Lieutenant H. did not know. He was stunned, completely bewildered. It happened that Belle had also asked him to carry a small package for her, which he had politely pocketed without examining. This was unfortunate for him as this, too, was marked "Kindness of Lieutenant H."

The enraged colonel tore it open. The package contained a copy of the rebel newspaper, *The Maryland News Sheet.* That settled it. The hapless lieutenant was court-martialed and dismissed from the service. Belle, her important letter still clasped in her hand, returned home unscathed.

Back at Front Royal, Belle found a new arrival in her aunt's old home, a Mr. Clark, a reporter for the *New York Herald.* Like most of the men who met Belle, he was attracted to her. But Belle disliked him intensely. Sometimes she had to bolt her door in his face.

It was in May that rumors reached her that Stonewall Jackson and the Confederates were going to march on the town. Those observant eyes of hers saw that the Union men were working at top speed to remove their stores. And what she could not see for herself, of course, she learned from the indiscreet confidences of the Federal officers, who poured out their news to her sympathetic ears.

From a high window Belle watched the Confederates advance, three-quarters of a mile away, through opera glasses. Then, passing Mr. Clark's door, she grinned to herself, turned the key and locked him in his room.

"I had information," she wrote, "that would wrest victory out of defeat."

She knew what the strength of the Union troops was, what their plans were. She made up her mind to take the information to Jackson herself. This was probably to be Belle Boyd's major service for the Southern cause.

She was wearing a dark blue dress and a fancy white apron. She pulled on a white sunbonnet and began to run down the street. Before long she was within range of the Federal pickets who "fired on me. Bullets struck the ground throwing dust in my eyes." A little later, and that running figure, conspicuous in the white sunbonnet, was exposed to crossfire between Confederates and Federals.

As she came nearer to the advancing Confederate troops, she took off her sunbonnet and waved it over her head. What on earth, Jackson demanded, was that woman doing out there? An officer came out to see.

"Go back quick," she panted, "and tell Stonewall that the Yankee force is very small, one regiment of Maryland infantry, several pieces of artillery and several companies of cavalry. I went through the camp and got it out of an officer. Tell him to charge right down and he will catch them all."

General Jackson himself rode up to the breathless girl. Did

she need an escort home? No, she would go back as she had come.

The Confederate troops raced down on Front Royal, driving out the Federals.

"The day was ours," Belle related. "When I got back, exhausted, Confederates filing through the town greeted me with cheers."

To add to Belle's pleasure on that triumphant day, the obnoxious Mr. Clark, unable to escape from his locked room, was captured.

Belle herself finished the day by going to the hospital to dress wounds.

Thanks to Belle's intelligence, the Confederates not only saved the bridge but they took 3,000 prisoners and captured thousands of small arms and hundreds of thousands of dollars worth of supplies.

"I thank you," Stonewall Jackson wrote to Belle in a letter which remained her most cherished possession all her life, "for myself and for the Army, for the immense service that you have rendered your country today."

The victory, however, was of short duration. Before long, the Federal troops were back in town and it was the Confederates who had to withdraw. And, one day, there was a knock at the door. Three men were waiting for Miss Belle Boyd. They had come with orders from Secretary of War Stanton to arrest her and take her to the Old Capitol Prison in Washington.

Belle's clothing was searched. So was the house. Plenty of incriminating evidence was found, as caution was not the girl's strong point.

She entered the Old Capitol Prison just two months after

Mrs. Greenhow had been released to go South. It is hard to imagine a greater contrast then the one between these two famous women. Both were spies. Both were ardent Southerners. Both were exceptionally attractive to men. But the tempestuous Mrs. Greenhow was a born intriguer. Her stay at the Old Capitol had been a time of loud recriminations and complaints.

And Belle? The first general awareness of her presence was the sound of her voice, singing joyously and triumphantly, "Maryland, My Maryland."

Politely asked what the guards could do for her comfort, she demanded a fire and a rocking chair! As for the food, she had no complaints on that score. The daily menu, she said, included soup, beef steak, chicken, corn, tomatoes, irish stew, potatoes, bread, butter, canteloupes, peaches, pears, grapes.

In fact, Belle was having a wonderful time. She enjoyed everything. Her sense of humor made it all amusing. She described how, on Sundays, Superintendent Wood of the prison strolled along the corridor, "in the tones and with the gestures of a town-crier proclaiming: 'All of you who want to hear the word of God preached according to Jeff Davis, go down into the yard; and all of you who want to hear it preached according to Abe Lincoln go to Room 16.'"

Belle, defiantly wearing a small Confederate flag pinned to her dress, went gaily to the Sunday service in the yard, exchanging friendly greetings with other Confederate prisoners; even, according to one report, managing to become temporarily engaged to marry one of the prisoners! She brought sunshine and laughter and high spirits into the Old Capitol.

She hadn't been there long before she established contact with her fellow Secessionists. She wrote notes on tissue paper, wrapped them around marbles, and rolled them into the rooms of the other prisoners while the guard's back was turned.

After a fairly short imprisonment she was released and sent back to Richmond. Her reception was not unlike a contemporary ticker-tape parade. She was welcomed as a heroine, serenaded, showered with honors, reviewed troops. Among other honors she received "my commission as captain and honorary aide-de-camp of Stonewall Jackson."

At the General's suggestion, partly perhaps as a propaganda move, partly to keep the irrepressible girl out of trouble, she went to Knoxville, Tennessee, where she was forced to make a speech from a balcony to an enthusiastic crowd. That winter she seems to have spent being fêted and honored, going to parties and having a wonderful time. The culmination came the following spring when she made a tour of the South, which was, she recalled, "one long ovation."

After the battle of Gettysburg, the Federal troops were back in Martinsburg so Belle Boyd, unwittingly, found herself inside the Union lines once more. A new order came for her arrest. As her mother had a three-day-old baby she needed her daughter's care, so she appealed and for a month she was allowed to remain at home. But guards were stationed around the house and Belle was not allowed to receive visitors. She could not even step out on the balcony. This time they were going to take no chances.

When the month's respite had ended, Secretary of War Stanton renewed his order for Belle's arrest. This time she was taken to the Carrol Prison in Washington, an annex to the Old Capitol.

It took only a few days for Belle to discover a crack in the wall. She got to work on her side to make it large enough to push through tightly rolled notes to the prisoner in the next room. When this maneuver was discovered, the crack was sealed up and the prisoner moved to another room.

When a new prisoner took his place, Belle decided she could establish communications if she could pry off a board. As she had no tools she asked the guard to "lend me his bayonet." This the obliging fellow did! While she was at work, Superintendent Wood appeared at the end of the corridor and Belle leaped to hide the bayonet under the bed. The superintendent never observed that the guard was minus a bayonet.

Her last trick at the Carrol Prison was to help three prisoners escape. She consulted with them in some way and gave them $40. Two of them were in the garret of the Carrol, and one on the floor below where Belle was imprisoned. As the prisoner from Belle's floor was trying to get upstairs to join his friends, the guard saw him.

"Halt!"

Belle called out: "You haven't been here long enough to know where the prisoners belong."

The guard assumed he was mistaken and let the prisoner go up the stairs. Then Belle sent the guard with a note asking Superintendent Wood to come see her. She held his attention engaged until the signal for which she was waiting came.

From around the corner came a shout: "Murder!"

In the confusion, sentries ran wildly around to see what had happened, and Superintendent Wood looked out of Belle's window. On the other side of the building, the three Southerners took advantage of the confusion to climb out on the eaves, slide down a lightning-conductor and get away. They were next heard of, safe in Richmond.

Then the excitement and the fun suddenly palled. Belle Boyd was tried by court-martial and found guilty of espionage. She was sentenced to imprisonment at hard labor at Fortress Monroe for the duration of the war. She heard her sentence in stunned horror and then fainted.

She started for Fortress Monroe but before she reached there, her sentence was commuted to banishment to the South. Although she was relieved to reach Richmond, free, there was no happiness, even for this bright-hearted girl, for the first news she heard was of her father's death.

By this time, Belle Boyd was so well known that her usefulness was over. From now on, she was a danger to her cause as well as to herself. With President Davis's approval, she decided to go to England. She carried official dispatches with her, took the alias of "Mrs. Lewis," and set off on the blockade-runner *Greyhound*, commanded by Captain Henry, formerly of the U.S. Navy but no longer fighting for the Union cause.

They were at sea only a day before the *Greyhound* was fired on by the U.S.S. *Connecticut*, a Federal cruiser. The *Greyhound* was forced to surrender.

The prize master of the *Connecticut* was Lieutenant Hardinge, a Union naval officer.

"I know I am a prisoner," Belle told him with suspicious meekness.

"Consider yourself a passenger," the young lieutenant said gallantly.

Within the next few days Belle had impressed her captor so powerfully that he asked her to marry him. Belle did not commit herself but she didn't discourage him, either. "He might in future be useful to us," she wrote.

The *Connecticut* docked at New York and for a few days

the "captive" had her usual luck. The newspapers were all agog at the arrival of "the Confederacy's Cleopatra." Instead of being put in jail, she was given an excellent hotel room and both her captor and Captain Henry escorted her on a round of theaters and visits to friends.

Then she was taken to Boston. Before she arrived, Lieutenant Hardinge had proposed again. This time Belle said yes. But her activities were not yet over. Wherever she went she seemed to land on her own feet, but things might not go so smoothly for Captain Henry of the *Greyhound* who had left the Union service and changed sides.

When they had anchored off the Boston Navy Yard, Lieutenant Hardinge called to two Yankee pilots and asked them on board for a glass of wine. The lieutenant asked Belle what he had done with his papers. He had left them in the cabin, she said. While Hardinge went below for his papers, Captain Henry wandered across the deck. Once out of sight, he dropped into a boat and, by the time the hapless lieutenant arrived, he had escaped.

There was much excitement over the escape but again Belle managed to avoid punishment. For a few days she stayed at the Tremont Hotel. Hardinge took her sightseeing in Boston. Then the authorities clamped down. Belle Boyd was to leave at once for Canada.

"If I was caught again in the U.S. or by U.S. authorities I should be shot."

So Belle's activities as a spy came to an end. She had been in prison twice, arrested five or six times, and reported between twenty and thirty times.

In England, Belle reported to the Confederate States Commission. A few months later, Hardinge, who had been dismissed from the Navy for neglect of duty, joined her and they were married. After two months, he returned alone to the United States, carrying Confederate dispatches. He was arrested and imprisoned. His health broke and Belle had to sell her wedding presents to help him. To raise more money, she wrote *Belle Boyd in Camp and Prison* with assistance from a professional writer.

At twenty-one, she was a widow and the more spectacular part of her life was over. But Belle's zest for life and experience was never dimmed. In England, she went on the stage, playing in *The Lady of Lyons*. Later, once more back in the South, she appeared in stock companies or gave talks about her experiences as a spy. She was married twice more, once to an English officer and later to a Northerner from Ohio. She died in Wisconsin in 1900. Hers was a full life and, on the whole, a joyous one, for she was always high of heart.

EMMA E. EDMONDS,
MASQUERADER

AFTER the horrified picnickers, who had come to watch
the battle of Bull Run as though it were an athletic contest,
had fled homeward, a slight girl with a square face, untidy
hair and bright eyes remained on the battle field, doing what
she could to relieve the wounded and to ease the dying.

This was Emma Edmonds. She was a Canadian girl from
New Brunswick who had planned to become a foreign missionary. In 1856, her family moved to New England. A few
days after Fort Sumter she left for Washington and volunteered as a field nurse.

Emma was not a girl who was limited by circumstances.
When the supplies of fresh food for her patients ran out, she
went foraging, even if she had to go into enemy country to
find it for them. Once her request for food for her patients
was answered by a revolver bullet which narrowly missed
her. She had applied for help to a Southern woman who had
lost several members of her family in battle and hated all
Union sympathizers.

Tireless and determined, Emma continued with her search
for food. One of her leading characteristics seems to have been

the ability to make her own plans and operate on her own, a quality that is essential to a spy.

One day, she was returning to camp from such a trip when she met a group of soldiers who had just returned from burying a picket who had been killed while riding the line. The soldier whose grave had just been dug was the man Emma loved. After the initial shock and grief, she was no longer satisfied even with the exacting and dangerous job of field nurse. She wanted to do something more vital. Washington seemed to be filled with Southern spies. Perhaps there was something that she could do there for the North. She went to the chaplain and explained what she had in mind.

"That morning," she wrote later, in her account of her spy activities called *Nurse and Spy*, "a detachment of the Thirty-seventh New York had been sent out as scouts, and had returned bringing in several prisoners, who stated that one of the Federal spies had been captured at Richmond and was to be executed. This information proved to be correct, and we lost a valuable soldier for the secret service of the United States."

At her eager prodding, the chaplain went to headquarters and suggested that the nurse, Emma Edmonds, be used to replace the spy who had just been hung. Emma was summoned by General McClellan and examined on her fitness for spy work.

Psychological tests were unknown at that time. Instead, a phrenologist felt the bumps on her cranium. He declared that her organs of secretiveness, resourcefulness and combativeness were well developed.

Then she was questioned.

Why did she wish to undertake such dangerous work? She

wanted to be of service.

What was her attitude toward the war? She was strongly opposed to the institution of slavery.

Could she ride? Yes, she was an expert horsewoman.

Did she know anything about firearms? She was an excellent shot either with a carbine or a pistol.

McClellan must have hesitated. She was so slight in build. On the other hand, there was that determined jaw. Perhaps, after all, a girl who had been a field nurse under fire could handle the more dangerous assignment. It would be worth taking a chance.

The nurse was given three days to prepare to cross the Confederate lines at Yorktown. So Emma, who on the eleven trips she was to make through enemy lines adopted many disguises, prepared to use the most daring, spectacular and difficult masquerade of all.

She sent to Washington for a wig, bought a suit of plantation-style clothing, and had her head shaved by the company barber. Then she stained her head, face, neck, hands and arms black and pulled on the wig of Negro hair. She examined the result dubiously. So far as she could tell she looked like any young Negro man.

She practiced her speech and accent. The greatest danger in disguise, particularly one as spectacular as this one, is that a person may be taken by surprise and speak or act out of character.

Emma tested her disguise by seeking out her friends and talking to them. They not only failed to recognize the young nurse they knew; they never suspected that she was not a colored boy.

She slipped across the lines. All that she took with her was a revolver and a few hard crackers. The job assigned her was to learn anything she could about fortifications, troops and, if possible, the enemy plans.

"I started on foot," she wrote. "At twelve o'clock I was within the rebel lines . . . I had passed within less than 10 rods of a rebel picket and he had not seen me."

There was nothing to be accomplished in the dark. So Emma lay down on the ground, which was damp and chilly. There was no sleep for her. No telling what might lie ahead. She could only hope to grasp every opportunity to pick up intelligence. But would her disguise prove good enough? Lying on the wet ground in the chilly night, Emma did not feel like a bold spy. She was a very frightened girl.

Next morning, the light awakened her. In a short time, she encountered a Negro work party. This was the real test. Would they accept her as one of their own or would they detect the masquerade at once?

Her nerves must have tightened with fear. Then, unexpectedly, the slaves hailed her and kindly offered to share their coffee and corn bread with her. She had been accepted.

The white man in charge of this work party of 100 men issued orders. If she was to be fed she must help with the work of building defenses. So all day long Emma pushed a "monstrous" wheelbarrow filled with gravel up and down a narrow plank to an eight-foot parapet.

By the end of that day the girl was exhausted. She had performed heavier labor than she had ever known. Besides that, her hands were a mass of blisters from wrist to fingertip. But, tired as she was, she set out that night to saunter around and see what she could. With those painful hands she managed to make a sketch of the outer works and to list the armament.

Her notes she concealed in the inner soles of her work shoes. Next day, the work seemed more difficult than ever. Her muscles were sore and strained. Her raw hands caused her agony. Then she got a shock. One of the Negro workers looked at her, puzzled. Darned if that fellow wasn't turning white, he exclaimed. Emma decided she had better get away before her disguise faded entirely.

She found a colored water boy and offered him $5 to change places. He took over that "monstrous" wheelbarrow, which had to be pushed up that steep, narrow plank. She took the water bucket and drifted around the camp supplying the thirsty troops with drinking water. The bucket was heavy and her hands bled from carrying it but she learned a lot by listening to the careless talk around her. Who would worry about what a water boy overheard?

Emma memorized the facts she picked up. That day she learned how many reinforcements there were in camp and where they had come from.

As she drifted around the camp she saw a man she recognized. She had seen him before in the Union camp. He'd been a peddler then. Now he was giving the Southerners the information he had gathered for them. He'd had to shoot a man on the picket line, he said. Emma remembered the party of soldiers returning from the grave they had dug for the man she loved. Now she had more strength, more courage to go on.

On the third night, Emma was the "boy" assigned to carry supper to the men on the outer picket line. This line was not popular. It was only half a mile from the Union line and there was constant danger of being shot. One of the pickets had been killed and Emma was put on temporary guard duty. She was given a rifle and told to shoot if she saw anyone coming.

She waited until all was quiet. Then in the dark she slipped away and, in momentary danger of being shot by both sides, hid in a ditch until morning. Then she returned to her own lines.

"I made out my report," she said briefly. She also handed McClellan the rebel rifle, which was later turned over to a museum in Washington.

Removing the black stain from her raw hands must have been a painful process, for none of the pain-killers or soothing lotions of today existed at that time. Then Emma returned to her strenuous field nursing, following the troops as they moved on. An odd little figure she must have been, with her tired face and her shaven head on which the hair must have seemed to grow back slowly.

For her next spying trip Emma adopted a completely different disguise. This time she went as an Irish woman peddling cakes to the soldiers. Instead of the dialect of Negro slaves, this time she had to practice an Irish brogue.

At that time the bridges across the Chickahominy had not been finished so Emma Edmonds, carefully balancing her basket of cakes, swam the river on horseback and then sent her horse back.

It was a black night. She had come ashore at the edge of a swamp. She did not know where the Confederate lines were. She lay in the darkness, hearing nothing but the muted sounds of the night life around her, the whine of mosquitoes, the stirring of small animals. She must have followed those sounds wide-eyed. What was that? Or shuddered at unexpected movements. Snakes, perhaps? Her clothes were drenched and fever struck her. For three days she burned with fever and shook with chills.

When at last she was able to move, she had no difficulty in finding the Confederate line. All she had to do was to follow the sound of cannon. As she was walking toward that ominous sound, she came to a house that seemed to be deserted. Perhaps she'd find something to eat. What she found was a Confederate soldier who was dying of typhoid. He was alone and helpless.

Spy though she was, Emma was first and foremost a nurse. This man was not an enemy, he was a patient. So Emma nursed him as well as she could, comforting his last moments. Before he died he handed her his watch and asked her to give it to Major McKee, who was on Ewell's staff. When he died, the exhausted nurse dropped to sleep on the floor beside the dead.

She had not contemplated anything as dangerous as conversation with a Confederate officer. Her plans had been limited to lounging around the camp peddling her basketful of cakes, and listening to any talk she might pick up. The dead soldier's watch provided her with an unforeseen opportunity to penetrate to a higher level. It would, however, also make her more conspicuous. There were bound to be rebel spies at Yorktown and someone might recognize her. She must make her disguise much more complete than she had planned.

Emma hunted around the deserted house and found mustard, pepper, a pair of old green spectacles and a bottle of red ink. With these she was ready to put the finishing touches on her disguise.

"Of the mustard," she explained, "I made a strong plaster about the size of a dollar. I tied it on one side of my face. It blistered thoroughly. I cut off the blister and put on a large patch of black court plaster. With the ink I painted red lines about my eyes, and after giving my pale complexion a deep tinge of some ochre which I found in a closet, I put on my green glasses and my Irish cowl which came over my face about six inches and left for the nearest picket line."

She knew that the dead soldier's watch would provide her with the best of passports. When she got near the picket lines she added the last touch to her disguise. She rubbed the black pepper in her eyes to make them red and watery.

When she got to the picket she waved a piece of window curtain at him as a flag of truce. The picket was lonely and talkative so he settled down to chat with the Irish market woman. He told her the bridge had been completed and an attack was imminent. He also informed her of the number of batteries.

Headquarters was five miles away. When Emma arrived, she learned that McKee was not in camp. By this time her blistered face had become infected and she had to use ointment on it. Then she wandered around the camp peddling her cakes and talking with an Irish brogue. By the end of that day she knew where all the batteries were, how many men were on hand and what the battle plans were. Now she wanted to get back across the lines as quickly as possible with the important and urgent intelligence she had collected.

But there was still that watch to be delivered to Major McKee. Next day, the Major returned and Emma managed to see him. When she gave him the watch, the Major wept. The soldier had been his best friend. In return for her trouble in taking care of his friend and bringing him the watch, the Major offered her some money.

Emma refused. She knew at once she had made a mistake. She had aroused the distrust of the Southern officer. Why would a poor peddler refuse money?

She had to repair the mistake quickly. She could never forgive herself, she declared in a rich brogue, if she took money for doing her best for "that swate boy that's dead and gone."

So far so good. Emma had made a slip and recovered. But she was as far as ever from her own lines and she was in a hurry to hand over her intelligence. How was she going to manage it?

At last she thought of a plan. She offered to lead Major McKee to the deserted house where she had left his friend. McKee agreed. He lent her a horse so they could make the trip more quickly. Once mounted, Emma knew that she could get away. And so she did that night, in the dark. She returned to her own headquarters with valuable information. She also turned over to them the horse the Confederates had let her ride.

In between those eleven spying trips through the Confederate lines, Emma continued to serve as field nurse, often under fire, while she ministered to the wounded and the dying. As the war front shifted she saw many battles, from the first Bull Run to Williamsburg, Fair Oaks, the Seven Days, Antietam and Fredricksburg. She also, at least once, served in Federal uniform as an orderly, working under fire.

Her last trip as a spy was to be her high peak of achievement. The Union troops had seized Louisville. Emma, disguised as a country boy, got a job as a clerk in a Louisville store. This time, she was actually within her own lines. Her specific job was to uncover Southern spies.

Nothing much seemed to happen in the store but Emma was not a person to depend on circumstances. She created them. She told her Southern employer that he might increase his business if he let the new clerk sell merchandise in the camp itself. This was a fine idea and her boss readily consented.

Emma took along some pocket knives, suspenders, and other items and set out for the Confederate camp. She fell into conversation with as many soldiers as possible, asked harmless-sounding questions and used her eyes. By the end of two weeks she had learned of three spies who were now living among the Union troops.

To one of her new acquaintances Emma confided that she wanted to enlist in the Confederate army but she didn't know how to get through the Union lines.

Nothing easier, she was assured. There was a rebel spy who had been posing as a Union man, going back and forth constantly. She could go with him. Emma agreed to the plan and arranged to meet her guide. Then, with great caution, she got in touch with the Federal provost-marshal.

Next day, Emma was back in the store, a slim boy with uncombed hair and bright eyes in a pale face. Into the store sauntered the provost-marshal. He made a purchase. When she handed it to him Emma also slipped him a written message.

That night, Emma set out with the Confederate spy to go through the lines. Posing as an inexperienced country boy, she was greatly impressed by the work of a spy. She asked questions and the spy answered them boastfully. He not only told her how he worked, but he gave her the names of two other spies.

Just before they reached the lines, armed Federals surrounded and captured them. Emma was secretly released but the Rebel spy was shot at daybreak. So many Northern spies had been shot by the South that the original policy of leniency was no longer in force.

Then Emma ran into trouble. She must have had a quick

ear and a talent for reproducing accents accurately. She had been a Negro slave, an Irish peddler, a military orderly, an aide-de-camp, and now she had adopted the accent of a Southerner so convincingly that the Confederates, seeing this young Southern boy in civilian clothes demanded to know why he was not in uniform. As he had not joined the Southern army voluntarily, he would be conscripted. Emma was placed under guard and then, at the last moment, she was saved by the arrival of Union troops.

For two years, Emma had been both nurse and spy. She had been in constant danger. She had often been under fire in the thick of the battle. In her endless masquerade she had lived as many kinds of people, her appearance, her speech, her personality constantly changing. Fearless as she was, she knew that she could never be off-guard for a single moment, never speak one careless word. A shift in accent, the betrayal of more education than she professed to have, anything would betray her.

In some ways, it is probably not too much to say that no American spy in either the Revolution or the Civil War, spent as strenuous or exacting a two-year period. There had been danger but no glamour. A shaved head, raw and blistered hands, a great suppurating sore on her cheek, reddened and smarting eyes. Not for Emma the glamour of Mrs. Greenhow or the gaiety and light-heartedness of Belle Boyd. There are many ways of serving one's country and Emma had chosen one of the hardest.

And then, while nursing at Vicksburg, her health broke down. She was racked with fever. She who had nursed so many people was herself a patient. She lay helpless in her hospital bed.

"All my soldierly qualities seemed to have fled," she related. "I could do nothing but weep hour after hour."

She was commended for her heroic services to her country and then she retired to New England, where she wrote her memoirs, *Nurse and Spy*, which had a wide circulation as propaganda for the Union cause.

Missionary—nurse—Negro slave—Irish peddler—orderly —aide-de-camp—Southern country boy, and others. The long masquerade was finally over and Emma Edmonds lived out the rest of her life as herself.

WALTER BOWIE,
MASTER OF ESCAPE

"Have you seen Wat Bowie?"

Up and down Maryland went the Union men searching, asking their question over and over. They read out the description of the wanted rebel: "A tall man with brown hair, small nose, gray-blue eyes, high forehead, drooping mustache."

People shook their heads. They hadn't seen Wat Bowie. But when the detectives sent out by Colonel Baker of the secret service in Washington or the cavalry troops had gone on, the people laughed in delight. Everyone laughed about Wat Bowie, partly because he made such a pest of himself to the Federal forces and always got away, but mostly because Wat himself was always laughing. He got such fun out of it.

Walter Bowie was born in Prince George's County, Maryland, the oldest of nine children. His father was a lawyer and Wat followed in his footsteps. He began practicing law in Upper Marlboro, because the courthouse was there. There wasn't much time, however, for his profession. He had barely got into his stride when the Civil War began.

As an ardent and loyal Southerner, Wat looked around to see how he could be most useful. His home community was in a strategic position. Just across the river lay Washington. Annapolis was near by. A spy in the right place, as Napoleon had said, was worth 20,000 men in the field. So Wat set to work. Back and forth, he went to Washington, traveling by night. He carried mail, forwarding it as far as Richmond, collected medical supplies for the South, picked up intelligence about troop movements. He watched what was going on in Washington and Annapolis.

According to the wrathful Colonel Lafayette Baker, Wat not only raised squads of men for the Southern army but he smuggled them through the Federal lines to the South.

The maddening thing was that Wat always slipped out of the traps that were laid for him. He was as hard to hold as an eel. Just when they thought they had him, he disappeared, followed by a wave of laughter. "He got so much fun out of it," people said. He loved to "stir things up," as he said himself. When he had got his men through the lines or carried out information and supplies under the noses of the men who were looking for him, he would roar with laughter. Then, suddenly, he would vanish altogether for weeks, only to appear again when he had accomplished another *coup*.

Finally, the War Department in Washington decided that this man Bowie was too much of a trial to be borne. His activities had to stop. Men were assigned to find him and bring him back. This was no easy assignment. Wat had been born in this section of Maryland. He knew every foot of it, the swamps and the fields, any place where a man could hide undetected. Best of all, he knew the people, who were prepared to do anything to protect the safety of this quick-witted, adventurous, laughing man.

During 1862, the Federal detectives pursued him for months

but there was no trace. They were always too late. Then one night they learned that he had gone to call on a girl. This was no one-man job. It would take a number of men to catch and hold the elusive Wat, who could wriggle out of a bear trap.

The house was surrounded. When Wat realized it, he went up to the second story, opened a window as quietly as he could, and dropped to the ground. Unfortunately, he dropped right into the arms of one of the detectives.

There was consternation in Maryland. Word went out that Wat Bowie had been captured at last. He was taken to the Old Capitol Prison in Washington, where, after a trial, during which he refused to talk, he was sentenced to hang as a spy.

There was a month between the day of Wat's arrest and the date set for his execution, and his friends got busy working out a plan and collecting the money needed for bribery.

Then, the day before he was scheduled to die, he was permitted to have a visitor. His aunt, Mrs. Taylor, was allowed to come and bid him farewell. When she reached the Capitol, the guards, knowing Wat's uncanny ability to escape them, searched her carefully. No gun, no knife, no weapons or tools of any kind. They let her go in.

The two talked quietly under the watchful eyes of the guards. Their words were harmless, the visitor gave the prisoner nothing. Then she kissed him good-by and left. But there was one thing the guards did not see. When she kissed him, she slipped a bit of paper from her mouth to his.

As soon as his aunt had gone, escorted by the guard, Wat cautiously read the little note. That night, it told him, a Negro would bring him supper and leave his door unlocked. The light in the corridor would be put out at seven o'clock and a ladder would be propped up against the skylight.

Wat waited. A Negro brought his supper and went out without locking the door. In a short time the corridor light went out and there was a muffled bump as the ladder went into place. Like a flash Wat was out of his room and groping for the ladder in the dark corridor. Up he felt his way to the skylight and in a few minutes more he was out on the roof, shivering in the cold rain.

Cautiously he peered over the side. A sentry was passing. He waited until the steady beat of the footsteps had faded away and then he dropped heavily to the ground. In the mud and rain he slipped, spraining his ankle. He struggled to his feet but found he could not put his weight on his ankle.

The sound of his fall had startled the sentry who came back at a run.

The quick-witted Wat did not wait for the sentry's challenge. He yelled at him for help. What roads! What mud! He sputtered with rage over the way Washington streets were neglected. The situation was outrageous. No telling how badly he had been injured.

Then he asked the sentry to give him his arm. He had probably broken his leg in the slippery mud. Grumbling and irascible, he held the arm which the guard politely offered and limped down the road, clinging to it for support. When the sentry reached the end of his beat and had to turn back, Wat said crossly that he'd probably be able to get on by himself but that he'd never come back this way if he could help it. Which was undoubtedly true!

Wat, who for months had devised new ways every night of fooling the Federals and getting mail across the Potomac, had no difficulty in getting home. The story of his escape with the help of the sentry had people rocking with laughter all

137

over Prince George's County.

But Colonel Lafayette Baker wasn't laughing. If he had wanted the Southern spy before, he wanted him even more now. This time, he sent not only detectives but a group of cavalry to get Bowie and bring him back. That's when his description began to be spread far and wide, when the question began to be heard: "Have you seen Wat Bowie?"

The orders for his arrest were always marked: "Not to be found."

Meanwhile, Wat Bowie moved from one hide-out to another, always a step ahead of his pursuers. Until one morning he walked into a little clearing. Around a fire sat a group of armed men eating breakfast. At once Wat realized that this was the party of men who were searching for him. He could not retreat. As a lawyer, he believed attack was the best defense.

He went forward. "You're making mighty free with my rails," he said. He went on angrily. There was plenty of wood to be had if they wanted a fire. They had no right to burn his fence.

The men apologized awkwardly and asked him to join them for breakfast. He accepted. He couldn't very well do anything else.

They looked at him. A tall man with brown hair, small nose, gray-blue eyes, high forehead, drooping mustache.

"Have you seen Wat Bowie?"

Yes, Wat said, as a matter of fact he'd seen Bowie just the week before. At that time he'd been headed west.

Wat grinned. It was just as well, he said cheerfully, that he'd met the Federal men on his own land. Otherwise he might have been in trouble. Some people said he and Wat

Bowie looked a good bit alike.

He warned them about not burning any more of his fence and walked off. Once away, he must have doubled up with laughter. Moments like these, high with tension, charged with danger, requiring lightning decisions, were the ones that made the work of a spy "such fun" to Wat Bowie.

Wat continued with his risky work, collecting war information, smuggling men and mail across the lines, all through that winter, all through the next spring, until the summer of 1863. By this time, the legend of Wat Bowie had swelled to such a point that Northerners as well as Southerners believed he could not be captured.

And then one day the Federal searchers learned that Bowie was to be found in the house of some cousins of his named Waring. One of them, Elizabeth Dunhill Waring, discovered that the house was surrounded. She suggested that Wat hide behind the kitchen fireplace.

Not good enough, he decided. They would search everywhere. He wouldn't have a chance if he were hidden. Hidden? But suppose he stayed out in plain sight?

There was a Negro servant who brought him some of her clothes. Elizabeth provided burnt cork. When she admitted the searching party they examined, as Wat had foreseen, every nook and cranny of the house, inside closets, under beds, even tapping the walls. But there was no sign of Wat, no one but the Warings themselves and two Negro servants in the kitchen.

None the less, this was the house to which Wat had planned to come. The Union men were certain of their information. Perhaps they had come too early. They would wait.

It was a summer day and the men were overheated by their exertions. They wanted a drink of water. The two Negro women promptly got up, each taking a pail for the water. They had to go to the spring for it, Elizabeth explained hastily.

"You're pretty tall," one of the men commented.

The tall woman dropped her bucket in her terror. Her eyes rolled. The men laughed and let her go.

It was some time before the water was brought from the spring to the impatient, thirsty men. Only the short woman returned.

"Where's the tall one?"

They had scared her, the slave mumbled. She had run away.

In a flash the Union men realized that once more Wat Bowie had slipped through their hands.

For nearly another whole year Wat Bowie continued with his escapades, always uncaptured, always out of reach, the clear sound of his laughter echoing in a mocking way in the ears of his pursuers. But the net was tightening, they had come to know most of his hide-outs, his friends, his methods.

So, in 1864, before another summer came, Wat Bowie resolved to give up his one-man war and he joined Mosby's Rangers in Virginia. He was too much of a lone wolf ever to have been a good soldier in a regular army corps but in Mosby's group he soon distinguished himself as a guerrilla fighter and he was made a lieutenant. However, this fighting, exciting and dangerous as it was, did not satisfy Bowie's fertile and mischievous mind. He kept showering Mosby with wild ideas. He wanted to stir things up.

Then he evolved a grand idea. Let's kidnap the governor of Maryland. With his persuasive lawyer's tongue he talked Mosby into consent. With a group of seven volunteers, ranging from a boy of seventeen to Bowie himself, then thirty-one, they set out. But first they had to have horses. Nothing easier. Bowie knew where they could get plenty of horses. Where? From the Federal provost guard, of course. Only twelve miles away.

At Port Tobacco the eight men waited until all was still and the town was asleep. Twenty men of the provost guard slept in the courthouse. The eight Rangers stood at the door.

"We'll shoot the first man out."

Not a man moved. The Rangers stole the horses they needed and rode on to Annapolis to kidnap the governor. There the plan received an unexpected setback. Not only was the place heavily guarded but the governor was out of their reach. He had gone to Washington on a trip.

They started back. Perhaps his phenomenal success in making hairbreadth escapes had made Wat believe, as many other people did, that he led a charmed life. Anyhow, that night he was careless. He and his friends broke into a store and stole the food they needed. Only a short distance away, in a clump of pines, they settled down to have breakfast. Then, weary from their night's exertions, they stretched out on the ground to sleep.

They set no guard. While they slept, the horses they had taken from the provost guard were stolen from them.

They were awakened by the sounds of approaching troops. Their horses were gone. They were outnumbered.

One of the Rangers said uneasily, "There are too many."

"No, we'll fight." Bowie's laughter rang out. "We'll charge 'em on foot."

There was a shot that struck Bowie on the side of his head. He knew that it was fatal.

"Leave me," he called to his men in warning. And then, they related later, "He laughed like mad let loose."

So Wat Bowie died, as he had lived, with laughter on his lips. Gallant, brave, quick-witted, he served the cause he loved with all the qualities he had and he loved every minute of it.

ELIZABETH VAN LEW,
GRANT'S SPY IN RICHMOND

She was a tiny woman, thin and nervous, with a sharp nose, blond hair that, at forty, was fading like her youthful prettiness, and blue eyes of an "almost unearthly brilliance." This was Elizabeth Van Lew, "Miss Lizzie" to her neighbors in Richmond. Not, one might imagine, an heroic figure. But, in the words of General George Sharpe of the Army Intelligence Bureau: "For a long, long time she represented all that was left of the power of the United States Government in the city of Richmond."

How was it possible for this small, middle-aged woman to acquire such power, alone, unaided, hated and threatened, living for four years in the heart of the enemy camp? The answer seems to lie in her deep faith in the Union and a passionate belief that the enslaving of men was an evil which must be eradicated. But the saddest dilemma for this valiant woman was that she loved the South, she always regarded herself as a Southerner, and yet, by her own convictions, she had to live at odds with it.

It is easy to march into battle, surrounded by approving comrades who are doing the same thing. It is painful to walk alone, surrounded by the disapproval and the hatred of life-long friends and neighbors. No greater courage can be required of any human being.

Diagonally across the street from St. John's Church in Richmond, where Patrick Henry had once cried out, "Give me liberty or give me death," was the Van Lew mansion. In the midst of terraced gardens with boxwood hedges and magnolias, the great three-and-a-half story mansion with its tall Doric columns stood on Church Hill, one of the highest spots in Richmond. It was a magnificent house, with superb chandeliers, the parlor walls covered with brocaded silk. In it had been entertained many of the celebrities of the day: Jennie Lind, Chief Justice Marshall, Edgar Allan Poe.

The Van Lews lived, in those pre-war days, in great state. There were glittering balls and delightful garden parties. There were journeys to White Sulphur Springs, a fashionable resort, in a coach drawn by six white horses.

Elizabeth's father, a descendant of a Colonial Dutch family, had settled in Richmond in 1816, where he made and lost a fortune, and then started over again and made a second. His wife was the daughter of a former mayor of Philadelphia. So it was natural that Elizabeth should be sent to Philadelphia for her education. An abolitionist took her to the tobacco factories and Negro jails so she could see for herself the ugly results of slavery.

As a result of what she had seen, "Miss Lizzie" became, in her own words, "the unwavering abolitionist," declared that "Slave power degrades labor," and during the 1850's, some time before the war, she freed the slaves who belonged to the Van Lews. Most of them stayed on working for her. She also bought the husbands or wives of her former slaves, who had been in the hands of other owners, so that families might be reunited.

After the attack on Harper's Ferry, Miss Lizzie realized that there was small hope that a civil war could be prevented. An ardent patriot, who believed that love for the Union should be greater than that for a single section of it, she cast in her lot, without hesitation, for the Northern cause. At once she began writing letters to government officials in Washington, warning them of the attitude of the people of Richmond and explaining what the situation was.

As conditions worsened and the states began to secede, feeling mounted. The neighbors and friends who had long acknowledged the prestige of the Van Lews began to change their attitude. They no longer accepted the Union. They were Secessionists. But the Van Lews were still loyal to the Federal government. Suspicion and growing resentment turned to open hostility against them.

For her part, little Miss Van Lew, with her hair in ringlets and her bright blue eyes, was disturbed by their attitude. When she heard Southern women tell their men, "Kill as many Yankees as you can for me," she could not understand their lack of national patriotism.

Almost everyone longs for approval and popularity but the Van Lews did not hesitate. Elizabeth's mother was as staunch as she was. As for her brother, he refused defiantly to fight in the Confederate army. When he was impressed into service, he escaped to the Union side, taking valuable information with him.

Meantime, Elizabeth began collecting intelligence about troop movements and sending it across the lines. After the first battle of Bull Run, Richmond was filled with Northern prisoners.

Elizabeth asked for permission to visit the prisoners. At first, the suggestion was flatly refused. It wasn't fitting, she was told, for a Southern lady to visit these ruffians. "Such a crew wouldn't be fit for a lady to visit, ma'am." But she persisted. Surely she had heard the officer, only a few days before, talk on religion and charity. He relented and gave her written permission to "visit the prisoners and to send them books, luxuries, delicacies and what she may will."

This was a big stride forward. Libby Prison was a bleak, comfortless warehouse and Elizabeth Van Lew began to provide clothes, bedding and medicines for the prisoners. In time she persuaded the prison commander, Lieutenant Todd, a brother of Mrs. Lincoln, to send those who were seriously wounded to a hospital.

Amusingly enough, she worked on Lieutenant Todd's "kind feelings" by providing him with gingerbread and buttermilk, for which he had a weakness.

As Lieutenant Todd told Miss Lizzie frankly, she was the only woman who had offered to help the Northern prisoners. Her neighbors began to express their resentment openly. She and her mother were cut by their old friends and lived in almost complete isolation. The newspapers attacked them both savagely and threats began to be made against the two lonely women in the Van Lew mansion.

"We had threats of being driven away, threats of fire, and threats of death," Elizabeth wrote.

But the two women continued to spend as much money to help the prisoners as they spent on themselves. They provided money for legal counsel when Union prisoners were on trial, and gave money to those who needed it. Indeed, when the

146

four long years of war had ended, the Van Lews had spent everything they had, stripped themselves of money, to help the cause in which they believed.

Permission to visit the prisoners made it possible for Elizabeth to gain a great deal more intelligence than had been available through her own unaided efforts. In return, she took letters from them to smuggle through the lines to their families in the North. She also provided sanctuary for escaping prisoners in a secret room until means could be found to help them through the lines.

Years later, a niece of Miss Van Lew's, who had been a small girl at the time, told of hearing "Aunt Betty" moving softly about at night. The little girl stole after her. Miss Van Lew, candle in one hand, a tray laden with food in the other, went quietly up to the attic. She pushed away a box beneath the slope of the rear roof, slid open a panel and in the opening appeared a man's bearded face. The man reached avidly for the tray and the panel slid shut again, leaving him concealed in the secret room.

How many escaping prisoners Miss Van Lew hid in that room, at great risk to herself, no one will ever know.

For all her courage, Elizabeth Van Lew was never reckless. She used a cipher and kept the key to it, written in invisible ink, in her watch case. As far as possible, she managed to have no direct contact with her messengers. For instance, she used a pilaster with a loose top on one side of the fireplace in the library as a place to leave messages. One of her Negro servants would enter the room after she had left it, take out the message, slip it in his shoe and saunter away with it.

Naturally, because she had given them freedom and showed compassion in uniting them with their families, her servants were eager to help her. One of her cleverest tricks was to place Mary Elizabeth Bowser, a former slave whom she had not only freed but educated, in Jefferson Davis's own dining room as a waitress. Therefore, she had nightly intelligence regarding what was being said and planned by the Confederate President.

She reached out cautiously for people who could either provide intelligence or get it through the lines, by appealing to their patriotism or by using bribery. In time, she had farmers, government clerks, a seamstress, lawyers and many others working for her.

In many cases, as General Sharpe was to point out later, the Van Lews' "position, character and charities gave them a commanding influence and many families of plain people were decided and encouraged by them to remain true to the flag."

Through the Federal prisoners she learned about troop movements and supplies. When she was suspected of spying, permission was withdrawn for her to speak to the prisoners. So she brought them books to read. When the books came back to her, they contained small dots, which furnished intelligence.

Another way of circumventing the rule about not speaking to the prisoners was to hide messages in food containers. Miss Lizzie would carry a metal plate which had a double bottom to hold hot water and keep the food warm. She concealed messages in this lower part. Once, seeing that the guard looked suspicious, she prepared for her next visit. The guard insisted on examining the plate. Miss Van Lew instantly handed it to him. He pulled off the upper part. The lower part was filled with boiling water which burned him. After that, the guard displayed no further interest in the food-warmer.

As always in spy work, one of the chief difficulties was finding new methods of getting intelligence through the lines. One of Elizabeth's methods was to write her messages in cipher on thin paper and put it inside a scooped-out eggshell, which a farmer's wife took through the lines in a basket of eggs and fresh vegetables.

Another method was to have a dispatch worked in code into the pattern of a dress. The seamstress then carried it casually through the lines. A dress might be examined for hidden pockets but no one thought of studying the design.

In time, Elizabeth established contact with General Ben Butler at Fortress Monroe. Clerks in the Confederate War and Navy departments were furnishing her with almost daily intelligence.

Later, it was General Sharpe, in a letter he wrote to urge some financial compensation for Elizabeth Van Lew—a compensation she never received—, who summed up, in part, her activities during those four bitter years:

"The greater part of the military intelligence received from Richmond by the Army of the Potomac was collected and transmitted by Miss Van Lew. She established five secret stations for forwarding her cipher dispatches, a chain of relay points whose farther end was the headquarters of General George A. Sharpe . . . chief of the Bureau of Military Information, but the Richmond end of the chain was the old Van Lew mansion. There she received and harbored the secret agents who stole in from the Federal army; where no Federal agents could reach her she sent her own servants as messengers through the Confederate armies.

"There, in the Van Lew house, in the heart of Richmond,

she concealed many of the escaped Union prisoners from Castle Thunder, the Libby, and Belle Isle; there she planned aid for those who remained in the prisons, to whom she sent or carried food and books and clothing; for their relief she poured out her money—thousands of dollars—until all her convertible property was gone.

"Clerks in the Confederate War and Navy departments were in her confidence; counsel for Union sympathizers on trial by the Confederacy were employed by her money; for a long, long time she represented all that was left of the power of the United States Government in the city of Richmond."

While Miss Lizzie was going on with her dangerous work as a spy in Richmond, thirteen men had been arrested in New York, convicted of piracy and sentenced to hang. These men claimed they were Confederate privateersmen and therefore should be treated not as pirates but as prisoners of war. The Confederate government agreed, promptly threw thirteen Federal prisoners of war into a dungeon at Libby Prison and threatened that if the Southern prisoners were executed, the Northern officers would die in retaliation.

Miss Van Lew set to work, smuggled money in to the condemned men and smuggled out their letters to their families. Later, she was able to inform them that the thirteen Federal prisoners had once more been restored to their former status as prisoners of war. One of these men was Colonel Paul Revere of the Twentieth Massachusetts Regiment. It was because of her kindness to him that she was to be helped in her greatest need, many years later.

Elizabeth was constantly on guard. When she went to bed at night she always put beside her bed any dangerous documents so that she could destroy them at the first alarm. For, as time went on, her position became increasingly hazardous. To her former friends she was a renegade, a Southern woman who was disloyal to the South. Detectives began to follow her wherever she went. The house was constantly searched for papers or for escaping prisoners.

As the Southern cause worsened, she was the object of increasingly violent threats.

"From the commencement of the war until its close my life was in continual jeopardy," she declared.

At length, "I went to Jefferson Davis himself to see if we could not obtain some protection."

By this time, Lieutenant Todd, who had been cajoled with presents of gingerbread and buttermilk, had been succeeded by Captain George Gibbs as keeper of the Libby Prison. Elizabeth suggested that he and his family board at the Van Lew mansion, and so obtained his official protection.

Even this, however, was not enough. There was still the constant suspicion of the authorities, the bitter hatred of the people. Elizabeth Van Lew turned over various ideas. Finally she hit on one that might save her, that would arouse ridicule but disarm suspicion.

When she appeared on the street her manner, little by little, began to change. At first, she hummed or sang to herself, then she began to talk to herself; then, her head tilted on one side, she chatted and laughed with some imaginary person.

"Crazy Bet" they began to call her. "Crazy Bet" with a basket on her arm, wandering along the street, an object of fun. "There comes Crazy Bet." Actually, there, in that odd little figure, smiling, simpering, talking to herself, walked the leader of the Union in Richmond, the most resourceful spy within the capital of the Confederacy. When other Federal spies went to Richmond, they reported to her to "take her orders."

Of course, such an impersonation had its own dangers. She had to be constantly on her guard for fear a careless word would betray the fact that she was as quick-witted as ever.

One day, she was walking down the street when a man paused beside her.

"I'm going through the lines tonight," he whispered.

Crazy Bet walked on, mumbling and humming, but her thoughts were whirling. Was this one of her own men? In that case, she could get out some intelligence she needed to send. Or was he an enemy testing her? The risk was too great. She made no reply and went away.

Next day, she saw the Confederate regiment marching through the streets. Among the men was the one who had approached her the day before. She drew a long breath of relief that she had not betrayed herself.

Of course, there was not always a messenger at hand to perform her secret missions. So, often at night, Crazy Bet dressed herself in buckskin leggings, a one-piece skirt, cotton waist, and a calico sunbonnet. Off she would go on horseback.

Then a clerk in a government office warned her that all privately owned horses were to be confiscated for the army. Elizabeth needed her horse for her work so she hid it in a smoke house. Discovering that the Confederates had learned where it was, she spread straw thickly on the floor of the library and led her horse up the stairs. There it remained while the grounds were searched in vain.

As the end of the war approached, Elizabeth Van Lew was in almost daily touch with General Grant. She claimed, indeed, that roses from her garden reached his breakfast table with the dew still on them.

"You sent me," Grant wrote her later, "the most valuable information received from Richmond during the war."

Then, as Grant prepared to enter Richmond, the people who had long hated the Van Lews for their loyalty to the Union besieged the house. They were going to burn it to the ground, they threatened.

She stood facing them, but not now as Crazy Bet. A tiny woman with faded ringlets and blazing eyes.

"Do it," she challenged them, "and yours will be burnt by noon."

They retreated. Then she raised on her own roof the first Federal flag to fly over Richmond for four years.

General Grant was aware that his spy in Richmond would be in great danger. To protect her he sent a special guard to the Van Lew house. The Stars and Stripes fluttered from the roof but where was Elizabeth Van Lew?

They found her at last in the capitol. She had run there as soon as the Confederate forces retreated. Her last service was to search for any documents that might have escaped burning and that would be useful to the Federal government.

One of Grant's first actions in Richmond was to call upon her. He was probably the last distinguished guest to the Van Lew mansion. When the war was over, the most painful years began. The people of Richmond never forgave Elizabeth for her loyalty to her country. She had risked her life over and over. She had endured the hatred and scorn of former friends. She had experienced the bitter humiliation of her impersonation of Mad Bet. She had given all the money she had to the cause she believed in.

But now and for all the rest of her life she was to know grinding poverty and—worst of all—loneliness. She was to be an outcast in the city she loved.

Soon after his inauguration as President, General Grant appointed her postmistress of Richmond, a position she held for eight years. After that, she had no work and no income. General Sharpe's attempt to get her some repayment of the thousands she had spent for her country was unsuccessful.

"I live," she wrote, "—and have lived for years—as entirely distinct from the citizens as if I were plague-stricken. Rarely, very rarely, is our doorbell ever rung."

When her mother died, there were not enough friends of the Van Lews in Richmond to serve as pallbearers.

The long bitter years dragged on, years when the silence was seldom broken by a human voice, almost never by a friendly one. At length, everything was gone but the lovely mansion, which no one would buy. She did not even have enough food. Somewhere there must be help. In desperation, she wrote to Colonel Paul Revere in Massachusetts, whom she had helped many years before in his hour of need. She had to borrow a stamp from a Negro in order to mail her letter.

Help came, promptly and generously, from grateful friends and relatives of Colonel Paul Revere. They provided her with an annuity until her death in 1900. It is pleasant to think that descendants of the first Revolutionary spy came to the assistance of the last spy of the Civil War.

It was these Massachusetts friends who placed the bronze tablet over her grave with the inscription:

> She risked everything that is dear to man—friends, fortune, comfort, health, life itself, all for the one absorbing desire of her heart—that slavery might be abolished and the Union preserved.

INDEX

155

ABOUT THE AUTHOR

Rae Foley is the pen name of a well-known critic and writer in several fields. As Rae Foley she will be recognized as the author of a number of mystery stories, including *It's Murder, Mr. Potter*, *Where Is Mary Bostwick?* and *Run for Your Life*.